"A great intro for newbies to the territory, complete-
mixed with personal advice on how to handle debt and emulate the mind-
set of the wealthy. A wonderful resource."

—Danielle Town, author of *New York Times* bestseller
Invested and founder of *The Invested Practice*

"Erin is uniquely capable of making even the most difficult-to-understand
financial concepts into something you actually want to talk about, and investing is no exception. If you are intimidated (or, frankly, bored) by the
idea of investing, let Erin prove you wrong on both counts with this fan-
tastic book."

—Chelsea Fagan, cofounder of The Financial Diet and
coauthor of *The Financial Diet*

"Erin delivers exactly what she promises in this easy-to-digest, conversa-
tional book. If you're a millennial who wants to invest but don't want a
boring tome to put you to sleep, this guide gets you started without drown-
ing you in technical jargon. 'Level Up' your money by reading this book!"

—Kristy Shen, cofounder of Millennial Revolution and
coauthor of *Quit Like a Millionaire*

"*Broke Millennial Takes On Investing* is the beginning investing book
you've been waiting for. Not only does she break down investing terms, but
she also explains 'the why' in a way that will resonate with millennials and
non-millennials alike. What most impressed me is Erin's ability to explain
how to invest in a way that is easy to understand and implement. As a former preschool teacher turned financial educator, I can say that this book
has all the hallmarks of a great, transformative read. If you're starting your
investing journey, bring this book along with you."

—Tiffany "The Budgetnista" Aliche

"Erin compares asset classes to craft beers. Need I say more? She explains investing in a way that's simple and easy-to-grasp without being simplistic. She entertains you with stories of Dutch tulips and Ask Jeeves, introduces you to new technologies, walks you through ethical investing, and explains the investment landscape so well, you'll feel like an expert by the time you finish reading this book."

—Paula Pant, founder of AffordAnything.com and host of the *Afford Anything* podcast

PRAISE FOR

Broke Millennial

"It's the youthful perspective that makes this book so refreshing. It's well written and researched by a millennial for millennials. You hear their voices and their concerns without the judgment, sarcasm, and superiority we older folks too often convey when we talk to young adults about money."

—*The Washington Post*

"Erin Lowry's *Broke Millennial* is a charismatic guide to personal finances for people seeking a modern, thorough introduction to the topic."

—*Refinery29*

"A new book about money that teens and millennials will actually read. . . . This not only has great insights and tips about handling money, but it's written in a casual, relatable way." —*Time*

BROKE MILLENNIAL

Takes On Investing

A Beginner's Guide to Leveling Up Your Money

Erin Lowry

A TarcherPerigee Book

tarcherperigee

An imprint of Penguin Random House LLC
penguinrandomhouse.com

TarcherPerigee with tp colophon is a registered trademark of Penguin Random House LLC.

Most TarcherPerigee books are available at special quantity discounts for bulk purchase for
sales promotions, premiums, fund-raising, and educational needs. Special books or book
excerpts also can be created to fit specific needs. For details, write: SpecialMarkets@
penguinrandomhouse.com.

Library of Congress Cataloging-in-Publication Data

Names: Lowry, Erin, author.
Title: Broke millennial takes on investing : a beginner's guide to leveling
  up your money / Erin Lowry.
Description: New York : TarcherPerigee, 2019. | Includes bibliographical
  references and index.
Identifiers: LCCN 2018050287| ISBN 9780143133643 (paperback) |
  ISBN 9780525505433 (ebook)
Subjects: LCSH: Finance, Personal. | Investments. | BISAC: BUSINESS &
  ECONOMICS / Personal Finance / Investing. | BUSINESS & ECONOMICS / Personal
  Finance / Money Management. | SELF-HELP / Personal Growth / Success.
Classification: LCC HG179 .L6963 2019 | DDC 332.6—dc23
LC record available at https://lccn.loc.gov/2018050287

Printed in the United States of America
10 9 8 7 6 5 4 3 2 1

To Peach, my partner in building wealth

Contents

Is This Book Right for You?

Hello there,

Are you someone who is already maxing out your 401(k), making use of multiple investment apps, running a net worth update once a quarter, and reading Morningstar's website for fun? Awesome! You're crushing the game and are certainly more than welcome to read this book, but it's probably fairly rudimentary for you.

Or are you a rookie investor who may not even know what a brokerage account is but really wants to learn how to level up your money game in order to build wealth? Great! Welcome to the perfect beginner investing book.

Infomercial-like start aside, this book is my response to all the emails, DMs, and tweets I've received since publishing my first book, *Broke Millennial: Stop Scraping By and Get Your Financial Life Together.* People got their financial lives together and then they wanted to do more, and "more" meant investing. But I couldn't just say, "Start investing," because then the next, logical question was "Okay, but seriously, how do I start?"

I pondered that same question myself once, and I found it more difficult to answer than it should've been. Too many of the investing books on the market are jargon-heavy, assume that the reader has a base-level understanding of the markets, or, frankly, don't address Millennial-specific pain points like whether it makes sense to invest while paying off a student loan. (Yeah, there's an entire chapter dedicated to that question in this book.)

There will be jargon in this book. There will be stats and numbers. But we're also going to take things from what I consider the actual beginning: determining if now is truly the right time for you to start investing. We'll talk it out, and if it's not the right moment, then this book will still be here for you when you're ready.

If it *is* time, well, you've got 221 pages of fun waiting for you.

Yours in building wealth,
Erin

Introduction

The Case for Investing

ON A MILD summer day in Buffalo, New York, a simple conversation turned a risk-averse twenty-one-year-old woman into a bullish investor.

The year was 2010. America was just starting to pull out of one of the worst recessions since the Great Depression, but honestly, I couldn't have told you much about it. I was heading into my senior year and living in the spectacularly insular bubble that college so often tends to create. There were rumblings about it being tough out there for employment prospects, but as a journalism/theatre double major, I already had fairly low expectations. No one spoke of the housing crisis. People's parents were certainly being laid off, and yet that never trickled into dinners in the dining hall or late nights chatting in the dorms.

I was in the car with my dad. He drove while I sat shotgun. We were making small talk about the internship I'd worked that summer, which I'd accepted despite it initially being unpaid. To subsidize the cost of working for zero dollars, I saved up my resident assistant money, and I stocked up on pasta and Costco-size jars of peanut butter in preparation for scraping by. But a series of fortunate events transpired—namely, *The*

New York Times published a piece questioning the legality of unpaid internships, and the company where I was interning announced on my first day that interns would now be getting paid $9 an hour for our forty-hour work weeks. Eight weeks later, I had much of my initial savings left, plus the money from the internship itself.

I'd started watching *The Clark Howard Show* during lunch and breaks. Even though I'd been money-motivated from a young age, and an avid saver, I'd never read about or researched how to build wealth. I figured I would just keep being a diligent saver (putting my money into a savings account) and keep working hard until I made a six-figure salary, and somehow the combination of those two things would mean I'd one day be wealthy.

Clark Howard mentioned in one of his episodes that it's smart for college-age kids earning taxable income to open up something called a Roth IRA.

That fact bubbled up in my brain as I told my dad how much money I'd managed to accumulate since I didn't have to raid all my savings to survive during the summer.

"A money show I watched mentioned it's a good idea for college students to open a Roth IRA. Should I do that?" I asked.

"Sure, it's never a bad idea to start investing early," he told me.

"Wait, that's investing?" I asked. "I thought it was a way to save for retirement or something."

"It is a way to save for retirement, but it's also investing," he explained.

"Oh, I'm not sure I'm ready to invest yet," I responded.

Then he told me a story about investing that still guides how I behave as an investor.

Before I share his story with you, it's important that you know I am generally a risk-averse person. I never went through a serious rebellious phase and rarely broke a rule at home or school. You couldn't even get me on a roller coaster until well into my teenage years. My brain, to this day, likes to quickly compute the consequences and figure out how to mitigate any fallout before I take a risk. Given this information, logic dictated that

I'd be a cautious investor. And I probably would've been, if not for the following story from my father.

"Here's what you need to understand about the stock market, Erin. It's cyclical. It goes up and it goes down, but you need to hang on when it goes down and wait for when it goes back up. In 2008, the stock market went through a big crash and remained volatile for a while. When that happened, some people panicked and tried to pull out their money by selling their investments. On paper, your mom and I lost a lot of money during the months the market was down. I say 'on paper,' because we didn't *sell* those investments. We held on to them. Instead of panicking, we actually put *more* money in the market. When it's down, that's usually a good time to buy, because the stocks are essentially on sale. Then you just wait for things to turn around. Today, we not only have back what we lost on paper when the market went down, but we have even more because we were able to buy more at a lower price."

IT'S OKAY IF a lot of what my dad told me sounds like jargon to you. I felt the same way on that summer day in 2010. I did, however, get the overall point: the market goes up and the market goes down, so you need to have a long-term vision for your investments. And I got the distinct feeling that investing was what I needed to do in order to become wealthy. It became apparent that working hard and having the optimistic belief that I'd one day make a lot of money wasn't an effective wealth-building strategy. After all, having a big salary doesn't always translate into wealth. High income earners can live paycheck to paycheck, too.

The story from my dad deliberately oversimplified how the stock market works. It wasn't until later that he explained how you need to be strategic and diversified in your investments so you can weather the ups and downs of the market. That it's important to have an emergency fund, make a budget, and live below your means so that you don't have to raid your investments when life sends you some curveballs. He later talked about the emotional reaction you'll have when you see the angry red numbers on the screen telling you your investments have gone down and your net worth isn't as high as it was yesterday. And it wasn't until later that I asked how to even pick investments and where to actually go to put money into the market.

That's what this book is for.

WELCOME TO THE true beginner's guide on how to start investing and building wealth. I'm hoping you opened this book because you have at least a vague interest in investing, but like so many investors before you, including myself, you just have absolutely no clue how to start.

Here's your first step. Quiet the inner voice that's telling you some version of these excuses:

> "You're too young to worry about investing. That's a grown-up thing. Like married with a house and a yard and a dog and a kid kinda grown-up."
> "You're not smart enough to figure this out."
> "You're too broke to be able to invest in the first place."

You are grown up enough. You are smart enough. And we'll get to whether it's the right financial move for you to start investing now.

The fastest way to silence that inner critic is to clap back with why you need to be investing.

WHY YOU NEED TO INVEST YOUR MONEY

The simplest reason is this: it's an efficient way to build wealth.

Seasoned investors, personal finance writers, financial advisors, and pretty much anyone doling out money advice will wax poetic on the advantages of starting young and being consistent as an investor. The reason for this isn't wishful thinking about what could've been if they'd only started sooner or been a little more aggressive with their contributions to the stock market. It's simple math.

Reason 1: Compound Interest

"Compound interest is the eighth wonder of the world. He who understands it, earns it. He who doesn't, pays it," Albert Einstein, allegedly, once remarked.

Regardless of which wise man (or woman) made the statement, truer words were never spoken. Compound interest and the principle of compounding are essential reasons why investing early and consistently are touted as the means of wealth creation.

In short, compound interest is earning interest on interest. In extremely simple terms, it works something like this:

On January 1, 2019, you invest $1,000 in an index fund. (We'll get to what that is shortly.) By December 31, 2019, you've earned an 8 percent rate of return, so a total of $1,080 is now in your account. Starting in 2020, you begin earning interest on the $1,080 in your account, not just on the initial $1,000 investment. In 2020, you earn a 6 percent return on your $1,080, so you now have $1,144.80 in your index fund. Year after year, your money compounds, and you earn interest on your interest.

An increase of $144.80 in two years might sound like chump change, but imagine how quickly you can take advantage of compounding if you're contributing to your investments monthly or even annually? In the scenario just described, you didn't put in another penny after the initial $1,000 investment and you still earned $144.80 in two years.

Or try this example:

Instead of starting with $1,000, you begin investing $100 per month in an index fund. Over the course of twenty years, with the fund receiving an average 7 percent return, you will have earned $49,194.59. It only would've amounted to about $24,000 if you'd put the same $100 in a basic savings account each month instead of investing it.

Investing allows you to take advantage of compound interest in a way that socking your money away in a savings account doesn't.

Reason 2: Inflation

"The idea is, you will not outperform inflation without investing," says Carrie Schwab-Pomerantz, president of the Charles Schwab Foundation, and senior vice president at Charles Schwab & Co., Inc. "What I mean by inflation is the natural rise of prices for goods."

A hundred dollars can't buy you as much today as it could've in 1989 or 1999 or even last year. Before you feel like contradicting me, let me say that obviously this isn't always true for every good on the market. Thanks to competition in certain sectors and advancements in both manufacturing and technology, there are items once inaccessible to the general masses that are affordable today. But when we're talking about inflation, we're really referring to purchasing power. It's why your grandparents could take a family of four out to a nice dinner for $5 in the 1950s, but today you can't buy a value meal at McDonald's for one person for $5. Having $100 in your bank account in 1989 would be equivalent to having $203.59[1] today, according to the Consumer Price Index Inflation Calculator from the United States Department of Labor.

Money nerds make a big deal about inflation because your money will essentially lose value over time if it isn't at least keeping pace with inflation. From January 2008 to January 2017, 2 percent represented a decent rule of thumb for what to expect inflation to be.[2]

Your money needs to keep up with inflation, especially when you're saving for long-term goals like retirement. Just putting that money in a savings account will erode your purchasing power because savings accounts don't offer great interest rates. Or, as it's more commonly called, annual percentage yield (APY). In 2019, many bank accounts only offer you a measly 0.01 percent APY. That means if you have $1,000 in savings, you'll get a whopping $0.10 in interest by the end of the year. Some banks offer higher rates, like 1.75 percent APY, which would net you $17.50 in interest, but that's still a pretty measly rate if that's where you're putting your entire life savings because you aren't investing.

Investing helps protect your money against inflation. Sure, there will be years of low returns, but the average annualized return of the stock market will (most likely, because I can't make promises about market performance) outperform inflation. We know this because we have decades and decades of data, and even factoring in terrible years, it still averages out to beat inflation. However, this argument does make the assumption that your investments are diversified over a variety of sectors and companies and are not all in a single stock. We'll get into what those terms mean in chapter 2.

Reason 3: Time

The earlier you start, the longer you have to let compound interest do its job for you, and the better you can weather the ups and downs of the market. And best of all, the less money you have to invest each year to meet your goal. Think that sounds suspicious?

Meet Jake and Stacey, twenty-six-year-olds who would like to retire at age sixty-two. They've just started new jobs, and neither one has ever invested or saved for retirement before. They each earn $50,000 a year, and their employer offers a 4 percent match on their 401(k)s.

Stacey enrolls right away, putting 4 percent of her salary ($2,000) in her 401(k) in order to get her full employer match (an additional $2,000). For simplicity's sake, let's say Stacey stays at the exact same salary for the next thirty-six years, and that she receives an average 7 percent return on her investments.

In thirty-six years, when Stacey is sixty-two, she'll have just shy of $600,000 in her 401(k).

Jake decides to wait until he's thirty-six to begin investing in his 401(k). That means ten years of employer matches left behind, which, before compound interest, is $20,000! Again, for simplicity's sake, we'll say Jake also stays at a stagnant $50,000 salary per year his whole career.

Jake tries to play catch-up and puts 10 percent of his $50,000 salary toward his 401(k). That's $5,000 a year from Jake + the $2,000 employer match he receives. He, too, receives an average 7 percent return on his investments.

In twenty-six years, when Jake is sixty-two and wants to retire, he'll have almost $481,000* in his 401(k).

Jake contributed $3,000 more per year to his 401(k) than Stacey did, yet he accrued approximately $119,000 less than Stacey because she started earlier.

The Jake and Stacey example highlights why time matters. The earlier you start, the less you have to invest each month or year in order to reach your goals. Trying to play catch-up later is much harder than most people think.

"What you forget when you're a young person is that you don't have a mortgage yet, you don't have a family yet. Your financial commitments are less, and you have flexibility, and making decisions may feel tough then, but it's easier to make [them] then than when you have a mortgage and a family," explains Julie Virta, senior financial advisor with Vanguard Personal Advisor Services®.

Even if you earn a lot more later in life, it doesn't always mean you'll

---

*The compound interest calculations performed in this book are done using my favorite online calculator, from the US Securities and Exchange Commission, which you can find here: https://www.investor.gov/additional-resources/free-financial-planning-tools/compound -interest-calculator.

have hundreds to thousands of spare dollars a month to try to catch up on the investing you should've done a decade ago.

But don't take it from me. The stock market itself is happy to explain.

A LOVE LETTER TO YOU, FROM THE STOCK MARKET

Dear Millennial Investor,

While reading The Wall Street Journal, *I came across an article[3] I found quite distressing. Apparently, your generation is flocking to my bastard cousin, real estate, in the hopes of securing its financial future. You're flippantly tossing around hurtful statements about how I "spook" you or how putting your money in my grasp is nothing more than gambling. I'm not some two-bit slot machine you pump full of quarters in Vegas. I'm the Stock Market, and I believe it's time the two of us have a little heart-to-heart.*

Yes, there have been times I caused panic and destruction. Your history books teach you about Black Tuesday, and your parents may have lost some money when I took a dive in 1987. Most of you are probably frightened by me because of what happened in 2008. I know I caused some of you to lose jobs, while others graduated from college to face crushing unemployment rates. It makes sense why you view me as a wicked witch trying to lure you into a gingerbread house only to throw you into a stew. However, this exaggeration makes it clear that you've probably spent more time debating whether to binge-watch the latest Netflix series all in one weekend than learning about me from reliable sources. Yes, there will be days I get volatile and cause your portfolio some pain, but if you have the patience and commitment to tame me, then we can grow together.

My dearest Millennial, you are in the unique position of having what every investor craves: time. Time is exactly what will make you the next Warren Buffett. (Well, that's a lie. Time can help, but few people can make me their bitch quite like Buffett.) Time is important because it helps you grow your wealth while surviving future drops in the market. Time alleviates the pressure to quickly amass money in the later years of your life so you can retire. In fact, you can retire earlier if you learn how to master investing in your twenties instead of your late thirties or, heaven forbid, your forties.

For those of you interested in keeping all your surplus money as cash in a savings account, I beg of you to think about the low interest rates. If you won't need that little nest egg for five or ten years, then why are you stuffing it under the proverbial mattress by putting it in a low-yield savings account? Your money is pitifully wasting away when it can be used to make more money!

While we're on the subject of diversifying, go ahead and invest in real estate, but keep some funds with me, too. The real estate market can burn you just as badly as the stock market. And even if real estate is doing well, it doesn't liquidate into cash particularly quickly when you're in a bind.

If you're willing to commit to this relationship and become a long-term investor, then we can do well together. You need to be able to handle your emotions and remember to buy low and sell high. When I take a dip, don't run away screaming. Instead, consider pumping more money into my waiting arms. While everyone else panics and sells, you can scoop up some cheap buys and watch as they begin to rise until you can sell high. Because the secret is: I'm a cyclical beast.

Your teachers probably told you that we should learn from history. Well, if your young brains are as open-minded as your generation claims they are, then learn from the history of investing. Those willing to establish a committed relationship with me through good times and bad, in sickness and in health, are handsomely rewarded. Those who run at the first sign of trouble will never amass the wealth I can make them.

So, my Millennial, I ask that you please reconsider your relationship with me. I can offer you both the danger of being with a bad boy and the power of being with one of the biggest players in the financial world. Plus, when you catch me on a good day, I'm really not too hard on the eyes.

My most sincere love and gratitude,
The Stock Market

WHY *I'M* THE ONE TALKING TO YOU ABOUT INVESTING

Okay, I've made my opening argument in the case of *Your Future Financial Health v. Your Reluctance to Invest.* The defense for the Stock Market is going to take a brief rest, and I'm going to make another case: why you should listen to me in the first place.

You might've noticed early in my narration that I tactfully threw in a nugget about being a journalism/theatre double major in college. Notice what's *not* bundled in with those super-practical majors? Finance. Business. Accounting. Really, anything that might sort of make sense for the author of a book about investing to have studied.

You know what else I don't have? A storied (or even mediocre) career working on Wall Street. Any sort of advanced certification, like Series 7, 63, or 79, or any other exam an investment advisor may need.

Basically, I'm probably a lot like you. I got a liberal arts degree. I've worked in a few different jobs and changed my career path more than once. I started off making very little money ($23,000 my first year living in New York City) and gradually worked my way into a position where I felt it was time to level up my financial life. The first experience I had with investing was through an employer-matched 401(k), and now I'm self-employed and only have myself to rely on.

Now that I might've completely disqualified myself in your eyes, let me explain some of what *does* qualify me to write this book.

I've been writing about money professionally and not professionally (*cough* wrote a blog *cough*) since 2013. I've also worked for a financial technology ("fintech") start-up that compared financial products for consumers. There, I developed a strong bullshit detector for when a bank or financial professional was peddling a less-than-desirable product. Then I wrote my first book, *Broke Millennial: Stop Scraping By and Get Your Financial Life Together.*

Before and since authoring that book, I've been able to gain access to, speak with, and learn from a lot of people with far more experience than I. Plus, I've been DIY investing since 2012. That's not a long track record by any means, but it does mean I've been where you are right now.

My goal with this book is to work as a translator. I've spent time in the trenches, done the research, spoken to professionals, and now I'm synthesizing all that information into an accessible, digestible book. I'm not promising you huge returns or that you'll be a millionaire in just a few years, and anyone who makes such claims is worthy of some suspicion.

What I'm promising is that this book will help lay the foundation for you to start to take control of your finances and begin building wealth. I also promise that you'll have a better understanding of how investing works, from both a technical and an emotional perspective.

There are lots of voices in this book other than mine because I'm not playing the role of expert here. I interviewed CEOs of investment firms, creators of robo-advisors and micro-investing apps, certified financial planners, wealth management advisors, and executives at brokerage firms.

It's also important to me that you know one more thing about me.

FULL TRANSPARENCY ABOUT ME

As mentioned previously, I am self-employed. Speaking engagements and writing are the primary ways in which I make my income. In addition, I've also done brand partnerships and/or worked as a spokesperson or influencer. At the time of this book's publication, I will have been working in this field for more than six years, which means I've worked with a lot of clients. Some of my clients for writing projects, speaking engagements, and spokesperson work are financial institutions. It would be really simple to go back through my social media feeds and do some digging on Google to link me to a variety of banks, apps, and investment companies. Instead, I'll be up front with you.

Some of the companies I've worked with are included in this book. The relationships I've cultivated with financial services companies made it easier for me to get access to high-level people and persuade them to go on record and talk about investing advice for this book. However, I am in no way endorsing or promoting any of the brands you'll read about here. I have received no compensation in any capacity from the people or companies interviewed for or mentioned in this book in exchange for their being included.

DISCLAIMER ON INVESTING ADVICE— BECAUSE IT'S A SENSITIVE SUBJECT

(And because lawyers advise that it's a good idea!)

This book is a guide to help you learn how investing works. The experts featured in it and I are not giving you prescriptive investing advice. In fact, I've mostly made up names of investment products in order to be clear that I'm not suggesting you go put money into a particular stock, bond, or mutual fund. There will be times I name specific funds or indices. When I do, I am not (or a quoted expert is not) giving you direct advice to go invest in that fund or index.

As I've mentioned a few times by this point, the stock market goes up and down. Choosing to invest does mean you will, at times, see your funds go down. The quoted experts and I offer no guarantees about the market's performance; nor do they or I assume liability if you choose to invest.

Now that all the legal jargon and disclaimers are out of the way . . .

FEELING MOTIVATED TO GET STARTED?

Good! But before you get overzealous and start shoving all your spare cash into investments, let's take some time to assess your overall financial situation. Investing is a critical part of building wealth, but first you must make sure that you have the proper foundation. As flight attendants always remind us, "You must put your oxygen mask on yourself first before assisting others." Do you have your financial oxygen mask on? We'll find out in chapter 1.

Chapter 1

But Are *You* Ready to Start Investing?

THERE I SAT, staring at my phone, willing it to light up with a text message. It was fall 2011 and, shockingly, I wasn't a young woman hoping a boy would follow up about setting another date. Oh, no. It felt much worse than that. I was a financially desperate twenty-three-year-old trying to make ends meet in New York City, one who was hoping that, through sheer force of will, I could make one of the parents for whom I babysat respond to the feelers I'd just sent out.

"Are you free on Friday or Saturday evening?" the mother of my favorite babysitting charge texted.

"Yes, either one works for me," I wrote back within a few seconds, suppressing the urge to end with the colon-plus-parenthesis smiley face. It would have added desperation.

"Great, let's do Friday at six p.m.," she responded an agonizing twenty minutes later.

Friday at six p.m. meant I'd probably earn $120. This mom paid $20 an hour, and usually stayed out until at least midnight on her ladies' nights out.

I logged in to my bank account and assessed the rather pitiful state of affairs. At the time, I worked three jobs. My main job was as a page for the *Late Show with David Letterman*. The job, while fun, certainly didn't cover even my most basic living expenses: food, MetroCard, rent, cell phone bill. So, I had to subsidize it by babysitting and working as a barista. These three jobs usually resulted in me working from around 5:00 a.m. to 11:00 p.m. six or seven days a week. All those hours, and I still barely grossed $23,000 my first year out of college.

The brief story of how I made this work without sinking into debt involves finding ample free (or frugal) entertainment and living off of a lot of coffee shop leftovers (products that had passed their sell-by date but weren't expired), rice and vegetables, and the snacks fed to the little kids I babysat. That, and I'd stashed away a $10,000 buffer in college because of my obsessive pursuit to live in New York City after graduation. That buffer never ended up getting touched (after I raided it for the security deposit on my first apartment), but it was a significant emergency fund to have during a financially stressful time. I also knew I had the privilege of being able to call my parents if anything went truly, truly wrong. The parental safety net isn't one I ever used, but even its existence enabled me to take more career risks than peers who were not in a similar situation.

Worrying each month about making enough to be able to pay all my bills without dipping into my cash reserves didn't exactly put me in a prime position to start investing. Even though I'd learned some basics about investing already from my dad, I knew it wouldn't be wise to put anything in the market quite yet. Every penny I earned needed to go toward other, short-term financial goals. I needed to be able to put on my financial oxygen mask before taking any risks with my money.

GETTING YOUR FINANCIAL LIFE together is step one on the journey to becoming an investor. You also need to shake the common misconception that investing is just for the wealthy.

INVESTING ISN'T JUST FOR WEALTHY PEOPLE

"[T]here's this misconception that you need to be in a certain place before you can start investing," explains Jennifer Barrett, chief education officer for Acorns, the saving and investing app. "That was true when I was in my twenties, too. I sort of had this idea that investing was for the wealthy or investing was for the financially successful, which meant I had to get my stuff together before I could really go in big. I think a lot of people feel that way because it's intimidating and, at least in the past, you had to have $500 to $5,000 to open an account, so you really *did* need to have some money set aside outside of savings that could be used for investing."

Barrett touches on a real concern for most rookie investors: how much does it take to start? In some cases, you will be faced with a minimum amount to buy into a fund. For example, you may need as much as $3,000 to open an S&P 500 index fund with certain brokerages. Saving up $3,000 just to gain entry to investing can be a ludicrous scenario for some.

Fortunately, technology really has changed the game, and now the average rookie and seasoned investor alike have more choices and can start with much lower thresholds than available to previous generations. The much-touted index fund wasn't even created until 1976.[1] That may sound like a long time ago to your average Millennial, but consider that the New York Stock Exchange has existed as a formal organization since the 1800s. Chapter 8 will take a deeper dive into how technology allows you to get into the game without hefty minimum initial investments.

INVESTING ISN'T JUST FOR OLDER PEOPLE

As you continue on your journey to learn more about investing, there will be one common mistake that gets mentioned time and time again. "I'd say the biggest mistake is not starting early," explains Julie Virta, senior financial advisor with Vanguard Personal Advisor Services®. "The earlier you start, the better."

There are plenty of other mistakes you can make as a rookie investor, and we'll address those throughout this book, but believing you're too young to start is the simplest one to fix when you're young. In theory.

PUTTING ON YOUR FINANCIAL OXYGEN MASK

In reality, it can take years to get your financial life together, and while it's a mistake to wait too long to start investing, it's also a big mistake to throw your money into the market before you've taken the time to put your financial oxygen mask on first.

"You have to earn the right to invest," says Douglas A. Boneparth, CFP®, New York City's financial advisor for Millennials, and president of Bone Fide Wealth. "Investments are the sexiest part of personal finance, but it's just one piece." He adds, "There are a number of boxes you should be checking off before you find yourself putting risk on your money."

Ready to Start Investing Checklist

❑ Set financial goals:

- What do you want to achieve in the short, medium, and long term, and what will it take to get you there?
- Boneparth's rule: "For goals that will take four years or less to achieve, you are not putting risk on that money. You are not investing that money. Investing equals risk." We'll discuss goal setting further in chapter 4.

❑ Master cash flow:

- How much money is coming in and how much is going out? (Another, often hated-on term for cash flow is *budgeting*.)
- Can you easily pay all your bills each month? If you're still

in the "scraping by" phase, then it's not time to focus on investing yet.

- Boneparth explains that mastering cash flow allows you to figure out and be honest about what is a comfortable lifestyle, which is completely subjective, and enables you to become disciplined with your savings. But what's practical isn't always what's the most enjoyable. "Fun scale quite low, importance scale super high. Mastering cash flow must be done before you even contemplate investing," says Boneparth.

❏ Set aside cash reserves for your emergency fund *and* short-term goals:

- *For an emergency fund*: A fully funded emergency savings account is critical before you start investing. This money needs to be liquid, easily accessible, and "principal protected," according to Boneparth. "Principal protected" means you are guaranteed a certain return (like the interest rate on your savings account). Money that's invested isn't guaranteed a return, and you could end up with less than what you initially put in.

  Three to six months' worth of living expenses is the rule of thumb, but depending on your risk tolerance, you may want a little more cushion if you're self-employed or have a volatile income. Having three to six months' worth of money saved may sound like an insurmountable feat before you start investing. Before you panic, consider that this needs to only be your bare-bones budget. Not enough to keep you in your current lifestyle, assuming it's a comfortable one, but enough to keep the lights on, cover rent or mortgage payments, and put food on the table and gas in the car or a MetroCard in your hand.

It doesn't hurt to tack on a buffer fund for pets. My pup has his own (much smaller) emergency fund.

- *For planned upcoming short-term purchases:* This ties back to the first step on your checklist: "Set financial goals." Virta advises setting aside cash-flow needs for the upcoming six months before putting money in a long-term investment plan. This means not only your healthy emergency savings fund, but also any big purchases you may need to make or anticipated life changes (for example, moving).

❏ Pay off consumer debt:

- Any form of high-interest debt like credit cards, payday loans, title loans, and the like need to be paid off before you start investing.

- Mortgages and low-interest-rate auto loans are more akin to student loans. You must be current on your debt, but you don't necessarily need to have paid these off in order to start investing.

❏ Ensure student loans are current, if not paid off:

- Chapter 5 is dedicated to the "student loan debt and investing" conversation, so that should give you a sense that it's probably okay to start investing while you have student loans. There is nuance as to whether it makes sense, of course, but for the sake of your checklist, you need to be current on all your student loans before you've "earned the right," as Boneparth says, to start investing.

❏ Educate yourself about the stock market:

- Well, you're reading this book! That's a great place to start. Hopefully you can come back to this page and put a big checkmark here when you've finished reading it.

❏ Start saving for retirement:

- Saving for retirement is a bit of a misnomer, in my opinion. You should be *investing* for retirement. Putting money into a 401(k) or IRA means you are *investing*, assuming you don't have that money sitting as cash. We just don't tend to think of ourselves as investors when all we have are retirement accounts. But putting money into an employer-matched retirement plan or into IRAs should be your first foray into investing, which we'll discuss further in chapter 4.

  Yes, even if you have debt, you should be contributing to your employer-matched retirement plan. "The one exception to 'earning the right to investing' is getting free matching money. Obviously, go get that. If putting in 3 percent gets you 3 percent and you're going to stick around for a year or two, go get that free money," says Boneparth.

  To keep driving home the saving-for-retirement mantra . . . "Investing in a 401(k) should be a no-brainer, something you definitely do. So, if you work for an employer that has a 401(k) plan, you definitely want to invest in it, especially if that employer is doing a match. So, for example, if they're matching 3 or 4 percent, you should do at least that, minimum, to start. Those are dollars that are going to come out of your paycheck right away, before you even see them, so it's a great vehicle to start the saving. You don't necessarily see those dollars come into your pocket and then have to make the decision as to what to do with them. Getting your savings up to 15 percent of your income is ideal, especially if you plan for a higher lifestyle in the future or an earlier retirement," says Julie Virta.

Once You're Ready to Start . . .

- ▪ "Starting early and staying disciplined are the two primary focuses for a young person," says Virta.
- ▪ One way to stay disciplined is to automate! Decide on a sum of money you can comfortably invest each month. Then set up your brokerage to automatically pull it out of your checking account and put it in the stock market.

AM I TOO MUCH OF A BROKE MILLENNIAL TO START INVESTING?

You picked up this book excited to learn more about investing so you could get started, but after reading the checklist, you have a few unmarked boxes. Does that mean you can't invest yet?

Unfortunately, outside of contributing to retirement accounts, it does. It's important to lay the foundation first before you begin putting money in the market. Without the proper foundation, you can put yourself at greater risk in what is already a somewhat risky situation. Investing is a critical part of building wealth, but as Boneparth says, you must earn the right to start.

When You're Not Ready to Start Investing

- ❑ You haven't set financial goals:
  - Thinking "I want to be debt free" doesn't count as a financial goal. A financial goal needs to be both specific and actionable, such as "I want to pay off my $35,000 of student loan debt in the next five years."

- ❑ You still have credit card debt:
  - Student loans (potentially) get a pass (we'll discuss this more in chapter 5), but credit card debt needs to be paid off before you start investing.

❑ You don't have emergency savings:

- Three months' worth, at minimum, of your essential monthly expenses needs to be in a savings account. Don't tie money up in the market until you have this buffer.

❑ You haven't taken the time to learn about how the stock market works:

- You're fixing that one right now!

❑ You haven't started contributing to an employer-matched retirement plan, if it's available:

- Your first focus should be getting that employer-match. It's essentially a guaranteed return on your investment. If you don't have access to an employer-sponsored plan with a match, then you should still consider a retirement account as your first investment before planning to invest elsewhere. We'll discuss this more in chapter 4.

If any of these boxes get a checkmark, then you need to press Pause on investing. Take the time to put your financial oxygen mask on first. At the risk of being too self-serving, I suggest you start by reading *Broke Millennial: Stop Scraping By and Get Your Financial Life Together*. It will help you lay that necessary foundation in order to start investing. That's why this is the *second* book in the series!

That being said, I'm not telling you to stop reading this book. You can learn about investing before you've built your emergency fund, paid off your credit cards, or set all your financial goals.

HOW THIS BOOK IS ORGANIZED

The introduction has explained why it's important to invest your money and not just stash it in savings, and now you've figured out whether now is the right time to actually begin investing. In the words of Douglas Boneparth, you've "earned the right to invest." Or you've realized it isn't time for you to be putting money into the stock market (outside of retirement plans), but you still want to learn.

Akin to the style of the first book in the Broke Millennial series, this book does not have to be read cover to cover. Each chapter stands on its own, but I do advise you to read chapter 2 before progressing so we're speaking the same language.

However, just because you can skip around doesn't mean you should. I've created three categories of potential readers and recommended chapters based on your level.

The True Rookie

You've never dabbled in investing but are eager to learn more. Well, maybe not so much *eager*, but you've been told it's important, and this book seems like a way to ease in. You probably don't contribute to an employer-matched retirement plan yet or an IRA, and it's also totally okay if you don't know what either of those terms mean.

For the true rookie investor, it would be best to read this book in chronological order, chapters 2 through 9. (I'm assuming you've already read the introduction and this chapter, but if you randomly opened up to this page, go back and start at the beginning!) After that, you'll have a solid foundation and can begin to jump around based on your personal interests or where you are in your investing journey.

Chapter 2: Let's Establish a Common Language
Chapter 3: Grabbing the Bull by the Horns When You're Risk Averse
Chapter 4: I Have a 401(k)—Do I Need to Do More Investing?
Chapter 5: Should I Invest When I Have Student Loans?
Chapter 6: I Want to Put Money in the Market—How Do I Start?
Chapter 7: I Like Gambling—Isn't That Like Individual Stock Picking?

Chapter 8: Investing—Of Course There's an App for That
Chapter 9: Robo-Advisor or Human Advisor—Which Is Better?

Got Some Game, but Looking to Level Up

You've started contributing to your employer-matched retirement plan (or you contribute to an IRA), and maybe you've downloaded an app or two that're helping you dabble in investing. But you know you can do more and want to level up your current investing strategy. For you, I recommend:

Chapter 4: I Have a 401(k)—Do I Need to Do More Investing?
Chapter 8: Investing—Of Course There's an App for That
Chapter 11: Riding Out the Panic of a Market Crash
Chapter 12: Sniffing Out a Scam
Chapter 14: Tactics the Wealthy Use to Make and Preserve Money
Chapter 15: Where Can I Get More Investing Advice (Because I've Been on Reddit . . .)?

Want to Keep Learning
(and Maybe Feel a Little Smug About Being Ahead of the Curve)

As mentioned in the preface, this book is designed for beginners. I won't be taking you on a deep dive into cryptocurrency or providing a blueprint for individual stock picking (granted, the concept is addressed in chapter 7). Also, I won't make it easier for you to understand "hedgies" (the colloquial term for people who work at hedge funds) or any other term you may overhear at happy hour. There are well-written books available for you to learn about all those things.

Have you already opened your own brokerage account and contribute to your 401(k) and dabble a bit in investing apps and are thinking about hiring a financial advisor? Don't worry, there is still some value for you in this book.

Chapters that will interest you include:

Chapter 9: Robo-Advisor or Human Advisor—Which Is Better?

Chapter 10: Impact Investing—Making Money Without Compromising Your Ethics or Religious Beliefs

Chapter 12: Sniffing Out a Scam

Chapter 14: Tactics the Wealthy Use to Make and Preserve Money

Buckle up, it's time to move on to deciphering investing jargon. I promise to make this as painless as possible.

Chapter 2

Let's Establish a Common Language

SITTING IN MR. FUGAMI's eighth-grade Algebra class, I propped my head up by resting my chin on my hand, my eyes furtively darting to the clock above the door. In an effort to exercise some self-control, I played a game with myself to see how long I could go without checking the time. Three whole minutes later, I glanced over to see I still had another twenty-five minutes of class to get through before I'd be released to scurry over to Global History class. At least there I understood what was going on.

It was only a few weeks into the new school year, and it'd become clear that algebra would essentially require that I learn a foreign language. Hell, learning Kanji in my Japanese class had felt more doable than trying to remember that an *expression* is a group of terms and the terms are separated by an *operator* and that the pesky x or y symbol is really called a *variable* and that the number in front of the variable is actually called a *coefficient*.

Would I seriously ever need to know this in real life?

No, I've never needed to solve an algebraic equation for any of my jobs or in day-to-day life. But I did develop an appreciation for why I needed to understand those terms. Algebra needed a self-contained language in order to establish a common way to communicate. Plus, algebra became a whole lot easier once I could understand the necessary vocabulary.

INVESTING IS NOT unlike Mr. Fugami's Algebra class. It will feel intimidating and overwhelming at first. Just reading an article, listening to a podcast, or watching a YouTube tutorial on Investing 101 requires stopping to look up multiple terms before you can even get a basic grasp of what's being said.

Here's what usually happens (inspired by quite a few similar conversations I've seen in comments on blogs and in forums like Reddit):

ROOKIE INVESTOR: I have $2,000 I've saved up to put into the stock market. What should I do?

WELL-INTENTIONED RESPONDER WITH INVESTING EXPERIENCE: Assuming you're in a financial situation to start investing and are already saving for retirement, it's probably best if you look into investing using a taxable account and then dump your money into an S&P 500 or Total Stock Market index fund with an expense ratio of 0.04 percent, although that expense ratio might be difficult if you're investing only $2,000.

ROOKIE INVESTOR: Um, I understood the word *investing* and then got confused.

This is why the next step (after assessing that you're ready to start investing) is to learn the common language used both in the rest of this book and also so you can decode what people like the "well-intentioned responder with investing experience" above are saying to you.

This chapter is going to explain common investing terms in three categories:

1. What you absolutely need to know.
2. Things worth knowing once you get started.
3. Theories.

I'm going to do a deep dive into some of these definitions to ensure we're speaking the same language as we move throughout the book. Sometimes details are necessary when talking investments.

AN APOLOGETIC DISCLAIMER

Before you begin to frantically read the list of terms below and feel your eyes glaze over while your brain screams, "Whyyyyy?" I will make a small apology. A lot of these definitions require using another word that needs to be defined in order to explain the first term. For example, in the sentence "Asset allocation requires you to assess your risk tolerance and time horizon," you don't necessarily know what *risk tolerance* or *time horizon* mean. That's all detailed here, so be patient. This process will require some bopping around until it all begins to come together. The terms below are also in a specific order to try to minimize the pain of using one term to define another.

WHAT YOU ABSOLUTELY NEED TO KNOW

This may sound silly, but one of the first things you need to understand about investing is what exactly the term *investing* means.

"I think the common [definition] is putting your money in the stock market versus something that I would've liked to hear: putting your money to work for you," Kelly Lannan, a director at Fidelity Investments, told me. Lannan explained that reframing how you think about investing can help change your perception of investing. Besides, putting your money in the stock market itself isn't the only way you could be investing. Plenty of people pursue a real-estate-heavy portfolio in lieu of exclusively investing in the stock market.

Okay, now it's time to get serious about deciphering these terms.

ASSET CLASS: An asset class is a grouping of similar investments. It's like saying IPA, lager, ale, and stout are all beer. Beer would be the asset class with IPA, lager, ale, and stout being the similar investments. Equities (stocks), bonds, cash and cash equivalents, and real estate and/or commodities are the main types of asset classes. For example: if you put money into an S&P 500 index fund, then you've bought into the equities asset class. Then, if you buy a municipal bond, you've now purchased two asset classes: equities and bonds.

PORTFOLIO: The term used to refer to your investments or the grouping of your investments. "I haven't checked my portfolio today" means "I haven't logged in to my account to look at the details of my investments." It could be an all-encompassing term or may refer to something specific, like your real estate portfolio or your stock portfolio.

PUBLIC OR PUBLICLY TRADED: When a company "goes public," that means it is no longer just owned solely by the creator of the company or a close inner circle of friends, family, or venture capitalists. Now it is publicly available for the general public to buy a piece of the company by purchasing stock.

EQUITIES/STOCK: Here's a fun quirk: *equities*, *stock*, and *shares* are often used interchangeably. *Equities* and *stock* can be used as synonyms. Saying you own equities or hearing a term like *equity investments* means owning stock. But what does it mean to own stock?

In simple terms, owning stock means you own a piece of the company, albeit probably a very small one. You could be entitled to voting rights at shareholder meetings depending on the type of stock you own. You can also receive dividends as the result of owning stock.

Why would a company want to allow the public access to ownership? The reasons vary, but usually because the company is looking to raise money to either grow, pay off debts, or both.

SHARES: Shares are what your stock is divided into. When Jackie tells me she owns stocks, I'd take that to mean that she owns stock in multiple companies. If Jackie tells me she owns shares, then I'd ask, "In what company do you own shares?" While this isn't exactly a "you say tomato, I say tomahto" situation, it often feels that way. Both *stocks* and *shares* refer to ownership of a company. There is a technical difference between stocks and shares, but finding the difference hazy won't be detrimental to your ability to invest in or understand the stock market.

SHAREHOLDER AND STOCKHOLDER: *Shareholder* and *stockholder* mean essentially the same thing: you own shares of a company's stock. You can split hairs about the technical differences, but honestly, it's just not necessary for the purposes of this book. Shareholder tends to be the more commonly used term.

SECURITIES: You will also hear the term *security* or *securities* used to describe holding equities (stocks) and debts (bonds, certificates of deposits, etc.). It technically refers to the proof you have that you own a particular investment.

BONDS: You own a piece of a corporation's or government's debt when you buy a bond. Bonds are considered a less risky investment compared to stocks. There is an agreed-upon interest rate (called "coupon" or "yield") that is paid to the bondholder at certain intervals, such as once or twice a year. Ultimately, the borrower will then repay the full debt to the bondholder once the agreed-upon term is up (known as "maturity").

FIXED INCOME: Fixed income investments are typically considered conservative investments because you can expect a set influx of cash.

Bonds are an example of fixed income. As a bondholder, you've lent money to a company or government, and in return, you expect to receive set payments in interest until the bond matures and you're repaid your initial investment. Individuals close to or in retirement tend to have a fixed-income-heavy portfolio. But like any investment, there is no 100 percent iron-clad guarantee. Your borrower could default or the interest rate could lose value (known as interest rate risk) if you wanted to sell before your bond reached maturity.

CASH AND CASH EQUIVALENTS: I'm sure you get the cash part, that money in your checking account and savings account. The money you can easily access today. (This accessibility is often referred to as liquidity.) *Cash equivalents* refers to money that you can easily access (aka is highly liquid) and is a low-risk investment. Certificates of deposit (CDs) are generally considered cash equivalents for an individual investor.

ASSET ALLOCATION: This is one of the most critical pieces to your investing life because it's part of what will help keep you sane and able to weather the panic when the stock market takes its many tumbles. Asset allocation is the process of deciding in which asset classes you should be investing and how much of your portfolio should go into each. You need to consider your time horizon (when you'll need the money), goals, and risk tolerance when determining your asset allocation.

DIVERSIFICATION: Ask most financial advisors for the most important term people need to know when learning about investing, and *diversification* will be one of the first three terms out of their mouths. Diversification is best described with the cliché "Don't put all your eggs in one basket." There are two ways to consider diversification in your portfolio:

1.   You don't want a single asset class. Don't leave all your money in cash, or just in stocks, or exclusively in bonds, or only own real estate.

2.   You want to diversify within an asset class. For example, you shouldn't invest all your money in a single stock or sector. Just because you use and love Amazon doesn't mean you should exclusively invest in Amazon stock. And just because you work in tech doesn't mean you should only invest in the tech sector. You want to invest in the stocks of many companies across different sectors.

SECTORS: Sectors are industries, such as health care, energy, tech, real estate, or utilities. Investing exclusively in Amazon would mean you own a single stock in a single sector: technology. Should Amazon's stock tank tomorrow, then you'd lose most of your money. By diversifying, you mitigate your risk for when a particular company or sector takes a hit.

TIME HORIZON: "What's your time horizon?" is just a fancy way of asking "When do you need the money?" Despite its simplicity, a time horizon is a critical piece of your investing plan. You should know your time horizon before making an investment because it both informs how much risk you should take and can help calm your nerves during the market's ups and downs. A downturn in the market should be something you can brush off if you're well diversified and won't need the money for a few decades. If you need that money near-term, then you've probably moved your investments to low-risk or even already over into cash because you knew your time horizon. Money that is being stashed away for retirement when you're in your twenties can be invested more aggressively than the funds you want to use as a down payment on a house in a decade, because your retirement money has a longer time horizon.

RISK TOLERANCE: This is the gut reaction you feel about the potential of losing money. Risk tolerance, especially when coupled with your time horizon, is a critical part of your investing plan. Having a *low risk tolerance*, better known as being *risk averse*, generally correlates with putting your money in investments with lower yields, like bonds. Having a *high risk tolerance* could mean you take too much risk and don't properly balance your portfolio. You may need to learn how to battle against your natural risk tolerance—no one likes losing money!

Here's an example of risk tolerance and time horizon in the investing world: Many portfolio allocation models offered by companies come with names like *aggressive, moderate,* and *conservative.* These names tie into both your risk tolerance and time horizon. *Aggressive* means you're willing to take more risk while *conservative* indicates you can't stomach losing money. *Aggressive* should also mean you have a longer time horizon and won't need access to your money in the short term, therefore giving your investments a chance to weather the ups and downs of the market. Conservative portfolios often are for shorter-term horizons and indicate that you'll need some or all of your money relatively soon, or that you want fixed income (e.g., being in retirement).

BROKERAGE: You've probably heard the term *broker* before. In the case of investing, a broker is the person (or firm) that buys and sells investments on your behalf in exchange for a fee or commission. Yes, it's essentially a middle man. When you hear the term *brokerage* or *brokerage firm*, it's generally referring to the company that does the buying and selling on your behalf. Brokerages include the likes of: Charles Schwab, TD Ameritrade, Vanguard, Edward Jones, Fidelity, Scottrade, Ally Invest, and E*Trade. That's not all of them by any means, but they're an example of what people mean by the word *brokerage*. It's imperative you know that not all brokerage firms are the same, and you need to do your due diligence before working with any person or institution.

BROKERAGE ACCOUNT: A brokerage account is where you deposit the money you want to invest. Your brokerage firm facilitates the purchases for you. There are two distinct types of brokerage accounts: full-service and discount.

Full-service firms are that typical Wall Street image. It's the suit-and-tie-wearing financial advisor who will likely require you to have a high asset minimum (we're talking double commas) and will charge a flat fee that's a percentage of your total portfolio under management. Despite the snark, I'm not implying that full-service firms are bad. In fact, you can get access to more investment options with a full-service brokerage firm, but it's unlikely they're a good fit for your average, rookie, just-getting-beyond-broke Millennial investor. It also makes sense that this is usually referred to as "wealth management."

"Discount" unfortunately sounds sketchy, but it's actually what the average DIY investors (which many rookies are) use. I use discount brokerage accounts. The discount firms are lower cost than full-service firms because you're usually not working directly with a financial advisor who is developing your investment plan one-on-one. You decide where you're investing and you place the trade, typically online. The brokerage just facilitates it for you. For example, you put in the order to invest $300 into an S&P 500 index fund, and the next time you log in to your account, you see that transaction reflected. Vanguard, Fidelity, and Charles Schwab are examples of firms that offer discount brokerage accounts—but this doesn't preclude them from also offering the full-service option.

The other way to break down brokerage accounts is as cash accounts and margin accounts. Cash accounts are what we focus on throughout this book. You deposit the money to make an investment, and your brokerage buys what you requested with the funds you have. Margin accounts involve you being able to borrow from your brokerage for investments you want to make while leveraging your existing portfolio as collateral. This is not a form of investing we'll discuss in this book.

ACTIVELY MANAGED: A professional, known as a portfolio or fund manager, is managing the investments directly by making decisions about when to buy, hold, and sell the investments within a fund. For further clarification, let's say there are 100 companies in a fund your portfolio manager is handling. One of the tech companies in that fund starts to underperform, so your portfolio manager sells the shares he's holding in that tech company and buys shares in a different tech company to replace them. The fund manager's goal is to outperform a given benchmark, such as the S&P's 500 index. Passively managed funds mirror these benchmarks, so ultimately a professional is also trying to beat a passively managed fund.

PASSIVELY MANAGED: There's no professional involved, and investments are automated to mirror a specific index in the market. Mirroring a specific index is also known as *indexing*.

INDEX: A way to measure the market's performance by just looking at a statistically significant portion. There are many indices, but two you'll commonly hear about for the US markets are the Dow Jones and the S&P 500. For example, the S&P 500 is an index of the stocks issued by 500 large, publicly traded companies.

EXPENSE RATIO: The expense ratio is the cost you, the shareholder, have to pay in order to help cover the operational costs the brokerage incurs to run a fund. It's generally noted as a percentage of the fund's assets. For example, if the expense ratio on a mutual fund in which you invest is 0.62 percent, then you'll pay $6.20 for every $1,000 invested, or $62 for every $10,000 invested.

It's a simple concept but a critical one, because it significantly impacts how much you actually earn over time.

RETURN ON INVESTMENT (ROI): You've probably heard this expression used regularly in real life because it doesn't just refer to the stock market. It's my husband's favorite money term, so he loves to joke about the ROI of everything, from buying tickets to a Broadway show to paying off student loans to buying organic milk. ROI can mean the return on spending your time to learn a new skill or to fix something in the home yourself versus hiring a professional. What's the ROI of waiting in the standby line for *Saturday Night Live* tickets for eight hours when you only have three days in New York? But for the sake of this book, ROI will generally refer to how much you make on your investment relative to its cost. It's not just about how much your investment earned you, but what it actually earned you once you consider fees. The equation to figure out your ROI:

$$\frac{(Gain\ from\ investment - Cost\ of\ investment)}{Cost\ of\ investment}$$

MUTUAL FUND: You give your money to a professional who pools it with strangers' money in order to buy investments. It sounds shady, but that's actually the gist of what it means to own a mutual fund.

The less shady version goes something like this: Many investors don't have either the time to do the research or the money (capital) to buy the investments required to build a diversified portfolio on their own. Remember, you want to buy more than one stock and invest in more than one sector. You probably also want to own both stocks and bonds. Mutual funds give you that option, even if you don't have lots of money to start investing.

By using mutual funds, your money is being pooled with that of other investors to get access to investments you may otherwise not be able to afford on your own, because you can invest in hundreds, in some cases thousands, of securities at once with one mutual fund. Plus, a professional handles the research and builds the portfolio to try to get the best return for investors. However, because a professional is involved, the portfolio is actively managed, making the expense ratio higher than other options. This can eat away at some of your returns.

INDEX FUND: You still pool your money with strangers, but this time there's no professional involved. That might sound even crazier than a mutual fund. Index funds are under the umbrella of a mutual fund and work in a similar manner. You're combining with other investors' money in order to increase your purchasing power. The big difference between an index fund and a mutual fund is that an index fund is passively managed. Your investments mirror a particular index—hence the name—so there is no need for an active fund manager. Removing the professional does make the expense ratio lower, which makes it more affordable.

EXCHANGE-TRADED FUND (ETF): A hybrid option between mutual-fund investing and being able to buy and sell stocks. It makes sense to purchase this type of fund if you want to be able to trade instantly during the day, as you would with a stock. (Mutual fund transactions occur in bulk after the closing bell.) ETFs usually have pretty low expense ratios and lower minimums to buy in, making them attractive, but you also have to pay a commission to a broker each time you buy and sell. This could negate the advantage of a lower expense ratio.

COMPOUND INTEREST (COMPOUNDING): Compound interest is why investing early and consistently are touted as the easiest ways to build wealth. In short, compound interest is earning interest on interest.

Year 1: You invest $1,000 dollars in the Dogs Are Great index fund. The DAG fund earns an 8 percent return and you end the year with $1,080.

Year 2: You earn interest on $1,080, not the initial $1,000 you invested. This year, DAG earns a 12 percent return and you have $1,209.60.

If you'd just been earning 12 percent on the initial $1,000 investment instead of on the $1,080, then you would've earned $1,120. Combining year 1 returns of $80 with year 2 returns of $120 and simple interest (non-compounding interest) would've netted you $1,200 instead of compounding interest getting you $1,209.60.

A difference of less than $10 sounds low, but that's just in a year. Contextualize it over the span of decades and with more than $1,000. Compounding adds up, fast.

DIVIDEND: A payment you get from the company or fund in which you invested for being a shareholder. Dividends are a result of company earnings and generally get paid on a quarterly basis (i.e., every three months). Not all companies offer dividends, and dividends can be paid in various forms, such as cash or shares of stock. You can set up your dividends to automatically be reinvested.

DIVIDEND REINVESTMENT PLAN (DRIP): Instead of taking your cash dividend as a check or direct deposit into your bank account, you can use it to buy more shares. Usually, reinvesting your dividends comes without fees or commissions. That means you get a discount on your purchase because a fee doesn't chip away at your returns. It also creates a passive way for you to keep building on your investments with no thought required after you've opted in. You can often opt in to a DRIP when setting up your brokerage account.

THINGS WORTH KNOWING ONCE YOU GET STARTED

FIDUCIARY: Under the fiduciary standard, the financial professional or organization is ethically obligated to act in your best interest. Therefore, it is generally wise to work with a fiduciary.

SUITABILITY: Under the "suitability standard," a financial professional or organization is obligated to do only what is suitable and not harmful to you. The suitability standard has the potential to create a conflict of interest because the financial professional could direct you to invest in or purchase a product that earns the professional a commission or higher fee as opposed to the product that is best for you.

LOAD FUNDS: You pay a fee for the purchase (front-end load) or sale (back-end load) of your mutual fund investment. The fees for load funds usually pay the broker or advisor who researched the fund, advised you to purchase it, and placed the buy order for you. Back-end loads may be reduced or phased out, depending on how long you hold the fund. DIY investors typically avoid investing in load funds.

NO-LOAD FUNDS: There is no fee to buy into or sell your investment in this type of mutual fund. The expense ratios on no-load funds are typically lower than that of their load-fund counterparts. The fewer and lower the fees, the more you, the investor, pocket.

12B-1 FEE: Another fee your brokerage may charge for the operational cost of running a mutual fund. It is normally baked into the expense ratio, so you may not notice it at first, but it does push the overall cost up. The 12b-1 fee is capped at 1 percent by FINRA (Financial Industry Regulatory Authority).[1] That may not sound like much, but a 1 percent fee can really eat away at your returns, so check to see if a fund comes with a 12b-1 fee before making the purchase.

REBALANCING: Rebalancing is the process of buying and selling investments in your portfolio so the overall asset allocation is better aligned with your goals, time horizon, tax strategy, and risk tolerance. For example, let's say you have $40,000 invested in 60 percent stocks and 40 percent bonds in accordance with your time horizon and risk tolerance. The stock market did really well for three years, so the $24,000 you had invested in the stocks grew to $33,000 while the $16,000 in bonds rose only to $17,000. Now your portfolio is around 66 percent stocks and 34 percent bonds. You'll need to rebalance to get it back to 60/40. Generally, you want to rebalance at least once a year.

BULL MARKET/BEAR MARKET: A bull market means investments are on an upswing and prices are rising, which often makes people want to buy. A bear market means prices on investments are falling and people may lose confidence and start to sell. It is crucial to remember you will experience both bull and bear markets as an investor. The true guarantee of the stock market is that it's cyclical and will always go up and down, which is why setting your time horizon; having a balanced portfolio; and proceeding with your eye on a long-term, buy-and-hold mentality (i.e., don't panic and sell, sell, sell when the market dips) is a solid strategy. We'll dig into this more throughout the book.

CORRECTION: A correction is the downward trend of an index (e.g., the Dow Jones Industrial Average or S&P 500) or particular stock or commodity (e.g., cryptocurrency). Usually, *correction* is used when the value has dropped 10 percent or more. A correction can be an indicator that the stock market is heading for a bear market or even a recession, which is usually what you hear speculated in the media, but it's not a guarantee. From 2008 to 2018 there were six market corrections of 10 percent or more[2] on the S&P 500 index. Five of those corrections occurred after the Great Recession ended in June 2009. Corrections can also be a way to prevent a bubble.

BUBBLE: A bubble follows a simple pattern: A commodity becomes popular, and people get frenzied about buying in, thinking someone else will pay more for the item than they did. The price of the commodity hits a ceiling and people start selling, panic mode sets in, and the whole market around said commodity plummets. You probably even participated in a popular bubble from the 1990s . . . Beanie Babies!

Bubbles have been around for centuries. The classic bubble story money nerds like to tell is that of tulip mania, which swept Holland in 1637. In short, the Dutch got so crazy for tulip bulbs that it created a scarcity and thus supply and demand drove the prices up and up. Folks dumped their life savings and traded land in order to stockpile bulbs. Ultimately, as with all bubbles, it burst. People started to sell their stockpiled bulbs to actually cash in on their investments, which led to more and more people selling, which made prices plummet, and then more people panicked and tried to sell, which triggered a crash.

RECESSION: Millennials are no strangers to this term, considering that the Great Recession heavily impacted the career prospects and financial outlook of many in our generation. A recession is a period of more than a few months marked by negative economic growth and often manifests with slowed production and higher unemployment.

CAPITAL GAIN: Capital gain is investment jargon for making a profit on your investment by selling it for more than you paid. That profit doesn't occur until you actually sell your investment. Say you bought three shares of Broke Millennial stock for $2,500. In the first year, the investment went up from $2,500 to $3,200. But you don't sell. You hold the investment until five years later and decide to sell those three shares, which are valued at $5,000. When you sell those shares, your capital gain would be $2,500. You can get taxed on capital gains, aptly called a "capital gains tax."

TAX-LOSS HARVESTING: "Investments that you hold can go up and down. That's why we hold a number of different kinds of them and diversify them together. When they go down, the IRS has a bonus for you where you can save taxes by effectively taking a deduction for the losses. So the way you take that deduction is that you have to sell the investment. The trick, though, is you still want to be invested, so when you sell the investment you also want to buy back [a similar investment] to make sure you keep your portfolio in shape. *Tax-loss harvesting* is just a fancy term of looking for losses and taking the deduction to save you taxes," explains Alex Benke, CFP® and vice president of advice and investing at Betterment.

DOLLAR-COST AVERAGING: An investing strategy where you consistently contribute to an investment, often monthly, which means you're buying in at different price points, sometimes low, sometimes high. This can result in a lower average cost of your shares. Dollar-cost averaging also prevents you from trying to time the market and helps you ease in to investing. It's a strategy you'd already be using if you're investing into a 401(k) with each paycheck.

RETIREMENT TERMS

Are your eyes starting to glaze over a bit? There have been pages of terminology, so instead of dumping all the retirement talk into this chapter (and thus forcing you to flip back and forth), we're going to get into those in chapter 4, where we discuss retirement investing.

LET'S TALK ABOUT INVESTING THEORIES

You are going to hear about investing theories as you progress along your path to investing. Even something as simple as opening an investment app or checking out a robo-advisor will introduce you to terms like *modern portfolio theory* or *Monte Carlo simulation*. This begs the question: do I need to understand investment theories in order to start?

"No, complete waste of time," says Jill Schlesinger, CFP®, CBS News business analyst and author of *The Dumb Things Smart People Do with Their Money*.

I agree with Schlesinger, and in fact, we aren't going to talk about investing theories. There are entire books dedicated to specific investing theories, so we're not going to fall down that rabbit hole.

Instead, it's time to move on from learning a "foreign language" of investing to learning how to grab that bull by the horns—especially when *risk*, for you, is a four-letter word.

Chapter 3

Grabbing the Bull by the Horns When You're Risk Averse

"THEN I LOGGED ON and saw all the balances showed red numbers!" my friend Hazel bemoaned as we walked around our neighborhood park.

Hazel had started investing only about six weeks prior to our conversation. Despite taking quite a bit of risk in her career, which paid off, she self-identified as a risk-averse person when it came to her money. Hazel rationally understood *why* she should have some of her money in the market, but battled knee-jerk reactions to take her money out when those obnoxious, red, downward-pointing arrows showed up next to her investments.

I knew all this, which is why I responded by saying, "I texted you not to check your investments today. We're going through a market correction, so your investments were bound to take a tumble, but it'll be okay."

"Yeah, but I can't log in to my bank account without also seeing my investments," she shot back.

"Oh, yeah, that's a bit problematic," I acknowledged with a wry chuckle. "Are the investments at the top of the screen or the bottom when you log in?"

"Top," she said.

"Okay, I know this sounds silly, but what if you just cover your investment information with a sheet of paper or your hand when you log in to do your regular banking? That way, you aren't checking in on your investments, essentially against your will, on a weekly basis."

The recommendation sounds silly, but sometimes we have to set up this kind of barrier to protect our portfolios from ourselves. Frankly, *you* can be the biggest danger to your portfolio, especially if you have a low tolerance for risk.

The biggest issue with investing for both novice and seasoned investors is handling their emotions during market fluctuations. It's particularly difficult for risk-averse people to start investing at all and then leave well enough alone when the market starts to tumble. But it's important you learn how to grab the bull by the horns and avoid letting the bear intimidate you. Stock market puns!

YES, YOUR INVESTMENTS WILL GO DOWN AT SOME POINT

Remember in shows like *Fear Factor* how contestants underwent a perverse version of immersion therapy by completing awful tasks like being in a tank with snakes? While not as extreme, investing isn't completely dissimilar. You have to face your fear of losing money.

"The bottom line is the stock market does go up and down. That's just the nature of the stock market," says Carrie Schwab-Pomerantz, president of Charles Schwab Foundation, and senior vice president of Charles Schwab & Co., Inc. "But over the long term, it outperforms bonds and cash."

Of course, knowing this doesn't exactly keep you from having an emotional reaction.

"It's easy, when the markets are down, to get emotional about it and start pulling dollars out of the market when it's going down and putting dollars back in the market as it's rising," says Julie Virta, senior financial advisor with Vanguard Personal Advisor Services®.

The particular problem for many Millennials is that we grew up during the Great Recession. Kelly Lannan, director at Fidelity Investments, graduated from college in 2008, directly into the market downturn. "It was very scary seeing that, so as a result, I think we're naturally risk averse," acknowledges Lannan. "I think that Millennials are good savers, however, making that transition from taking something in your bank account that you can see every day, that's very safe, it's federally protected, and then putting it into an investment vehicle where there's much uncertainty, well, it can be hard to understand."

While the Great Recession may have caused some of the anxiety, it also provided a valuable lesson.

"The market was at an all-time high in 2007. When I say 'the market,' I mean the S&P 500 as a benchmark," says Schwab-Pomerantz. "Then, in 2008, it crashed 50 percent. So, if you had 1,000 bucks, all of a sudden it's $500 if it's in the S&P 500. But guess what? Not only has the stock market surpassed the 2008 number but also the 2007 number."

This real-life example demonstrates the importance of a buy-and-hold, long-term strategy when it comes to your investments. Had you been invested in the S&P 500 in 2008 when it dropped, and then sold, you would've not only lost $500 by selling, but also lost out on the gains of the market that rebounded and surpassed a previous all-time high.

HERE'S AN IMPORTANT SECRET TO KNOW

One of my professors liked to share a story about her neighbor. Her neighbor knew she worked in finance and liked to make small talk in the elevator by saying, "Guess how much I made on x, y, z stock yesterday?" My professor would always respond with the same line: "Oh, did you sell?"

The point of her story is that you haven't actually made a profit until you sell your investment and the money becomes liquid. The same is true on the other side of that scenario, when the stock market is taking a tumble.

"Hopefully, you won't panic and sell, because guess what? You're going to lock in your losses," says Schwab-Pomerantz.

This is why you'll hear both in this book and from many other investors that the buy-and-hold strategy is important. You should be playing the long game here, so if your portfolio drops because the market is going through a correction, or worse, a recession, then you haven't actually lost the money until you sell. And if you sell you have no opportunity to gain it back when the market goes back up.

WHY ASSET ALLOCATION AND DIVERSIFICATION ARE YOUR BESTIES

It's understandable if you feel like my friend Hazel. Investing in the stock market can be intimidating, not just because you don't totally understand how it works (yet), but because you don't want to lose money. That's where two important investing strategies come into play.

I asked many experts which terms they thought every rookie investor should know, and almost every single one said *asset allocation* and *diversification*. The reason these two terms are so critical is because understanding them and, more important, putting them into play will help mitigate the risk you take by investing your money in the stock market.

It's certainly not just rookies who use these strategies.

"[Asset allocation and diversification] are the investing strategies used by the largest pensions and funds in the United States," says Schwab-Pomerantz. "This whole notion of a well-diversified portfolio and using proper asset allocation of stocks, bonds, and cash—that's how the most successful investors have achieved their success."

Diversification is pretty simple to understand. You don't want to "put all your eggs in one basket." You don't want to invest in a single asset class—for example, don't leave all your money in cash or just in stocks or exclusively in bonds or only own real estate. Then you want to also diversify *within* an asset class—for example, don't invest only in a single company's stock.

The use of asset allocation is twofold, according to Jill Schlesinger, CFP®, CBS News business analyst and author of *The Dumb Things Smart People Do with Their Money*. "Over the long term, what you're hoping for is that different asset classes act in different ways over different periods of time. But, essentially, it's like hoping to protect you from yourself, because if you have 100 percent of your money in stocks, and the stock market drops by 20 percent, your $1,000 is $800. That might freak someone out. But if the stock market goes down by 20 percent, and only half of your money is in stocks, then if your $1,000 went to $900, it may feel more bearable. So, asset allocation is something that can really help people. What it also does is limit your upside sometimes, when the market is running away, but you have to be willing to make that deal with the devil. I'm willing to forgo some of my upside because the downside scares the shit out of me."

HOW DO I KNOW MY RISK TOLERANCE AND ASSET ALLOCATION?

We all love a good rule of thumb, especially when venturing into a new endeavor like investing. It helps simplify a potentially challenging situation. The rules of thumb in investing are plentiful, but that doesn't necessarily mean you should follow them.

A common one you're likely to hear is that (100)–(your age) = the percentage of your portfolio that should be invested in stocks. In my case, that's (100)–(29) = 71, so 71 percent of my portfolio should be invested in stocks.

But here's the rub: that doesn't account for my time horizon, goals, or risk tolerance.

"No, there is no rule of thumb," says Schlesinger. "Everyone wants there to be a rule of thumb, so there are shortcuts, but I think it's preposterous, in this day and age, that we're looking for rules of thumb when doing a very quick questionnaire online or going through an app that will take all of two minutes; we're still looking for shortcuts. The shortcut is that technology will do it for you."

Many brokerage firms offer free tools online for both customers and non-customers. You usually have to answer about ten to fifteen questions, and up will pop a recommendation for asset allocation that will be far more specific than a general rule of thumb. These questionnaires will also force you to really think critically about your investing strategy.

I typed "asset allocation calculator" into Google and found Vanguard's investor questionnaire in about fifteen seconds. The eleven-question questionnaire took me all of five minutes to complete and offered links to more information about what to know before reallocating and how my percentages compared to other allocation mixes.

HOW OFTEN SHOULD I CHECK ON MY INVESTMENTS?

Hazel had the misfortune of checking on her investments against her will simply because she needed to log in to her checking account. Checking on your investments frequently is not a good strategy for most people, regardless of their risk tolerance. "Don't look at your portfolio every day or several times a day. It's a long-term endeavor," says Schwab-Pomerantz.

"Generally speaking, six to twelve months," says Maria Bruno, CFP®, senior investment analyst at Vanguard Investment Strategy Group. "You don't want to do it too frequently, because basically you'll just [be] chasing your [own] tail—the markets do have bumps in the road and ups and downs." She adds, "At a minimum, check once a year. And pick an anniversary date."

Why do you need to even check in the first place if you have a buy-and-hold strategy, you may wonder? Because you'll eventually need to rebalance your portfolio to ensure that your overall asset allocation continues to be aligned with your goals, time horizon, tax strategy, and risk tolerance. If you purchased stocks and bonds with a 60/40 split and then the stocks performed really well, you could suddenly be at a 70/30 split, so you'll need to rebalance to get back to 60/40.

HOW TO PROTECT YOURSELF FROM YOURSELF

Ultimately, your biggest challenge is probably going to be learning how to put a line of defense in place so that you can protect yourself from yourself. Unfortunately, I don't know your exact idiosyncrasies to help make that happen, but here are some suggestions that may help uncover what can work for you.

Separate Your Bank and Investment Accounts

If you're anything like my friend Hazel, then you may want to invest with an institution that's separate from where you do your banking. Don't subject yourself to seeing what your portfolio is doing each time you need to access your checking or savings account.

Set Aside Cash in an Emergency Fund

"Always knowing you have a nest egg in emergency reserve will keep you from raiding that money you have invested for the long term," says Schlesinger. "Don't confuse your short-term, intermediate-term, and long-term money."

Assign a Goal-Related Name to Your Accounts

One of my favorite tactics is to nickname my savings accounts. Instead of seeing "Account no. 384841," I will change it to something like "Honeymoon: South Africa, 2019." Being specific reminds me why I'm saving and throws up a little psychological block in case I'm tempted to skim just a little off the top for an indulgence today.

Schlesinger recommends doing something similar when it comes to your investments. "If you keep those goals in mind and you say, 'It's in my retirement account,' that can be a really helpful way to prevent you from doing something dumb."

Automate Your Contributions

You may already have experience with automating contributions if you contribute to an employer-sponsored retirement plan. Setting up automation means one less thing on your to-do list each month, and it increases the likelihood that you'll consistently be investing money. Most brokerage firms have an option for setting up automatic investing that will pull your monthly contribution out of your checking account and put it into your investments.

Automating also provides a way for you to buy in to the market at various prices, a strategy known as dollar-cost averaging. "Dollar-cost averaging allows you to buy low when the market goes down and, obviously, you also buy when it's high, but you get a better price on average," says Schwab-Pomerantz.

Have a Plan

"The more you understand the market and the history of it, the more comfortable you'll be," says Schwab-Pomerantz. "Make an investing plan, stick with it, and try to avoid the noise. I remember 2008. It was such a scary time for all of us, even in the business, and I asked my advisor, 'So, Mike, the phones must be ringing off the hook.' And he said, 'Actually, Carrie, no. Everybody has their plan. They know their risk tolerance, they're well diversified, they know the market goes up and down, and they're staying committed to their plan. There's only one client who called, and he's just a nervous Nelly who always finds an excuse to call.' Having a plan and understanding it can help you ride out those ups and downs."

Hire a Pro

We'll discuss options for hiring help, but Schwab-Pomerantz recommends hiring a financial advisor if you need an accountability buddy or want the assistance. "I use a financial advisor. Even the pros get help," she says.

Don't Be Tempted by the Latest Hot Tip

"As humans there is greed and fear and following the herd. That's not what investing is about," says Schwab-Pomerantz. One of my favorite investing urban legends is that Joseph P. Kennedy Sr., father of John F. Kennedy Jr., famously sold his investments just days before Black Tuesday, when the stock market crashed in 1929. He claims that he knew it was time to get out because he'd received stock tips from his shoeshine boy. The line "When your shoeshine boy is giving you stock tips . . ." still gets used to this day.

There will always be the hot new stock or commodity everyone is talking about. From tulip bulbs to Beanie Babies to Bitcoin, it's just a reality of investing. You need to be careful about staying true to your own goals and plan. Any dabbling in the latest hot tip needs to be done with the speculative part of your portfolio that you can afford to lose.

WHAT IF YOU JUST CAN'T HANDLE ANY RISK?

Despite all this advice on how to mitigate risk and protect your portfolio from your knee-jerk reactions, you may still be coming to the conclusion that investing is just 100 percent not for you. The idea of putting your money in any investment, no matter how conservative, sends chills up your spine and a pit of nausea floods your stomach.

"Know that if you can't do it, it's not the worst thing in the world. It's just that you've got to save a lot more money," says Schlesinger. "Your money, when you invest it, is doing some of the lifting for you. When you're completely risk averse, it just means you're going to have to save a lot more money to reach your goals."

CHECKLIST FOR HANDLING RISK

❑ Embrace the fact that the market will go up and down.

❑ Put an investing plan in place that aligns with your risk tolerance but also helps you meet your goals.

❑ Understand the importance of asset allocation and diversification in your portfolio.

❑ Set up barriers to protect you from yourself when the market takes a tumble.

Chapter 4

I Have a 401(k)—
Do I Need to Do More Investing?

"THEN YOU CAN log in to the benefits portal and learn more about how to set up your 401(k) as well as your pre-tax transit card and health savings account."

I smiled tightly and nodded at my new manager as if I had any idea what she'd just said to me. The term *401(k)* sounded familiar, but those other two terms meant nothing. I made a mental note to call my parents after work and ask what those were and if I should use them. Then I returned my attention to the piles of starting-day paperwork and informational videos on office safety (even though the biggest threat I faced was a paper cut in this open-floor-plan public relations office).

A couple weeks later, I finally got around to evaluating my benefits package. The retirement package one-pager outlined that I'd get up to a 4 percent match from my employer and that the contribution would be vested immediately. There were two options: Roth and, from what I could tell, not-Roth.

Still a bit dazed from all these terms, I created a profile in an effort to be an adult and figure it out myself. That's when I found myself confronted with a scrolling list of investment options featuring names like *large cap*, *small cap*, and Dodge & Cox®.

Nope, this wasn't going to get figured out solo. So, I did what any enterprising twenty-three-year-old would do. I called my dad.

Surely his thirty-plus years in the business world would mean he could translate these terms into regular English, I thought to myself.

I was sort of right. He knew how to help me set the account up, but the man was so far along on his own investing journey that his attempt at simplifying the process still felt too complicated. But he did give me advice on which funds would create an aggressive portfolio in a Roth 401(k), given my long-term time horizon and, at the time, very low tax bracket. (It's okay if that last sentence overwhelms you. It meant little to me at the start of my investing journey, too.)

SAVING FOR RETIREMENT is not just important, but arguably it should be your first investing priority because:

- It helps lower your tax liability either today or in retirement.
- You're (possibly) getting free money from an employer.
- It can easily be automated, so building your nest egg is habitual, with minimal effort from you.
- You'll eventually want to achieve financial independence and be able to walk away from the *need* to earn a paycheck.

NOT SAVING FOR RETIREMENT YET?

If you're not saving for retirement yet, I'd like to point back to the example of Stacey and Jake in the introduction. Jake tried to catch up to Stacey after waiting ten years to start contributing to his 401(k). Stacey contributed only 4 percent of her salary in order to get the employer match. Jake contributed 10 percent, more than double what Stacey did, but he was still $100,000 behind her when they both retire at sixty-two.

Now, allow me to momentarily stay on my soapbox a bit longer and refer you to the following scenario and table to explain why it's imperative that you start now. Like, "Put this book down after my rant and go sign up for your 401(k) or open an IRA" kind of now.

> Assume twenty-one-year-old Kim saves $300 per month (or $3,600 per year) from now until she retires at age sixty-eight and receives a real rate of return of 4 percent. She would have approximately $500,000 at retirement. If Kim waits ten years to start saving, at thirty-one, she would need to save approximately $500 per month (or $6,000 per year) to achieve the same balance at retirement.

Assumptions:

Real Return	4.00%

Savings Annually	Savings Monthly	Balance after the following number of years							
		1	5	10	15	20	27	37	47
$1,200	$100	$1,200	$6,700	$14,800	$24,700	$36,800	$58,400	$101,800	$166,500
$1,800	$150	$1,800	$10,000	$22,200	$37,000	$55,200	$87,600	$152,700	$249,800
$2,400	$200	$2,500	$13,300	$29,500	$49,400	$73,600	$116,800	$203,600	$333,100
$3,000	$250	$3,100	$16,600	$36,900	$61,700	$92,000	$145,900	$254,500	$416,400
$3,600	$300	$3,700	$20,000	$44,300	$74,100	$110,400	$175,100	$305,400	$499,600
$4,200	$350	$4,300	$23,300	$51,700	$86,400	$128,800	$204,300	$356,300	$582,900
$4,800	$400	$4,900	$26,600	$59,100	$98,800	$147,200	$233,500	$407,200	$666,200
$5,400	$450	$5,500	$29,900	$66,500	$111,100	$165,600	$262,700	$458,100	$749,500
$6,000	$500	$6,100	$33,300	$73,900	$123,500	$184,000	$291,900	$509,000	$832,700
$6,600	$550	$6,700	$36,600	$81,300	$135,800	$202,400	$321,100	$559,900	$916,000
$7,200	$600	$7,400	$39,900	$88,600	$148,100	$220,800	$350,300	$610,800	$999,300
$7,800	$650	$8,000	$43,200	$96,000	$160,500	$239,200	$379,400	$661,700	$1,082,500
$8,400	$700	$8,600	$46,600	$103,400	$172,800	$257,600	$408,600	$712,600	$1,165,800
$9,000	$750	$9,200	$49,900	$11,080	$185,200	$276,000	$437,800	$763,500	$1,249,100
$9,600	$800	$9,800	$53,200	$11,8200	$197,500	$294,400	$467,000	$814,400	$1,332,400
$10,200	$850	$10,400	$56,500	$12,560	$209,900	$312,800	$496,200	$865,300	$1,415,600
$10,800	$900	$11,000	$59,900	$133,000	$222,200	$331,200	$525,400	$916,200	$1,498,900

Savings Annually	Savings Monthly	Balance after the following number of years							
		1	5	10	15	20	27	37	47
$11,400	$950	$11,700	$63,200	$140,400	$234,600	$349,600	$554,600	$967,100	$1,582,200
$12,000	$1,000	$12,300	$66,500	$147,700	$246,900	$368,000	$583,800	$1,018,000	$1,665,400

Table courtesy of Vanguard.

Compound interest. She's a beautiful, beautiful thing—when she's on your side. She's a real bitch when it comes to paying off debt.

SETTING UP YOUR FIRST RETIREMENT PLAN

A 401(k), 403(b), or IRA is often a person's first experience with investing. But just figuring out how to pick investments in a 401(k) can be dizzying, as I mentioned in my own experience. The paradox of choice can leave you frozen, akin to logging in to Netflix with the intention of finding a new show to watch and then defaulting to that same series you've watched all the way through at least four times.

Colleen Jaconetti, CFP®, a senior investment analyst for Vanguard Investment Strategy Group, explains the three simple steps you should take when setting up your first retirement plan:

Step One: Decide how much you want to save.
"At least try to save up to the point where you get the employer match," advises Jaconetti.

Step Two: Decide what types of investments you want.
"It's important to know what your time horizon is. Young folks will probably have a much longer time horizon, and generally speaking, the longer your time horizon, the more likely you can incur some kind of risk. Obviously, it's a personal decision, and people need to gauge their comfort with risk," says Jaconetti.

"... would recommend, if possible, for people to consider an all-in-one ... could have a balance of stocks and bonds, or some funds (like lifecycle funds) that would get more conservative through time. Those funds also rebalance themselves, so an important thing when you're figuring out what asset allocation you're comfortable with is sticking to that allocation through time. Generally, we would say people have to rebalance, but if you pick an all-in-one fund, you wouldn't have to worry about rebalancing. The fund would do it for you. If you pick a fund that becomes more conservative through time, then you don't have to consider when you want to become more conservative."

I should jump in here and mention that some financial advisors rail against the all-in-one fund (also known as the target-date fund). Historically, target-date funds have come with higher fees than when building your own portfolio, and in some cases, investors could find themselves invested at a risk level that doesn't align with their tolerance when nearing retirement. While the criticisms are all fair, the advantage of a target-date (aka all-in-one) fund is that it gets you started. It removes the overwhelming paradox of choice and makes sure your retirement money is invested in a manner that's somewhat aligned with your time horizon. Besides, you can always jump back into your portfolio in the future and rebalance or build your own once you're more confident in picking your own investments.

Step Three: Consider the costs of the funds.
"It's important to consider cost. It's not the most important factor, but it is a significant factor to figure out over the long term that every dollar you pay in fees is a dollar less you have for yourself or for future growth," says Jaconetti. "Some funds can charge higher fees, which just eats into the amount you have in retirement."

In chapter 6, we'll give a more comprehensive overview of fees, how to understand them, and the impact they have on your portfolio.

Now that you're convinced you must contribute to a retirement plan (or you're feeling smug about your decision to already do so), let's chat about those retirement-specific terms you should know that I promised to overview in chapter 2.

RETIREMENT TERMS YOU NEED TO KNOW

401(K) AND 403(B): Both 401(k)s and 403(b)s are retirement savings plans, typically offered by an employer, but 401(k)s are offered by for-profit companies and 403(b)s by nonprofits. Your company may offer only a traditional 401(k) or 403(b), but some, like my former employer, offer a Roth option as well.

- TRADITIONAL: Investing with pre-tax dollars up to the annual limit. You have the potential to lower your taxable liability today by contributing to a traditional retirement plan.

- ROTH: Investing with post-tax dollars up to the annual limit. The Roth 401(k) doesn't give you a tax advantage today, but you do get to withdraw the money tax-free in retirement.

You can generally invest in mutual funds, index funds, ETFs, company stock, bonds, and other forms of investments in your 401(k) or 403(b). Employers sometimes contribute to an employee's retirement plan, known as an employer match. You usually are required to contribute to the plan yourself in order to get the match from your employer.

EMPLOYER MATCH: One of the few terms that is just exactly like it sounds. Your employer puts money into your retirement plan, matching your contribution up to a certain percentage, but usually on the contingency that you contribute as well. For example: "We match you 100 percent up to 4 percent."

Say Hillary earns $40,000. In order to get her full 4 percent employer match, she must contribute at least 4 percent of her salary into her 401(k). That means she puts $61.54 per biweekly paycheck into her 401(k), and so does her employer. Hillary saves $1,600 a year in her 401(k) and receives an additional $1,600 from her employer, for a total of $3,200.

This is why you'll hear that failing to take advantage of an employer match is like leaving free money on the table.

VESTING SCHEDULE: Alas, sometimes an employer adds in fine print that the match will be subject to a vesting schedule. A vesting schedule determines when you'll actually be able to walk away with the money your employer is putting in your retirement account. Keep in mind that you get to keep the money you're putting in. The vesting schedule applies to the contributions your employer is making. There are three main types of vesting schedules:

1. *Immediate:* This is the ideal vesting schedule, which also makes it less common. The money is yours as soon as your employer matches your contribution. You could work there for three months and leave with the contributions your employer made.

2. *Cliff:* You will get all the money, as long as you wait out the vesting period. This could mean you need to work at the company for five years before you get to walk away with any of the employer match. But as soon as you hit your fifth anniversary, all that money has vested and is yours. If you leave before it's fully vested, you don't get any of the employer match.

3. *Graded:* A percentage of the employer match vests each year. Often it will go something like: 0 percent in year 1, 20 percent in year 2, 40 percent in year 3, and so on, until you're 100 percent vested. If you leave the company before reaching 100 percent, then you could take the eligible percentage. Say you left a job after three years and your employer had contributed $6,000 to your plan. You get to take 40 percent of $6,000, or $2,400.

Vesting schedules are used as a tool to retain employees because you may be incentivized to stay until the end of the vesting schedule.

If you don't stay, then it can save the company money, because when you forfeit the employer match, the money goes back to the company. Again, the money *you* contributed is yours to take. This only applies to the employer match.

TARGET-DATE (AKA ALL-IN-ONE) FUND: Target-date funds are a convenient way to save for retirement, especially when you feel overwhelmed about which investments to put in your 401(k), 403(b), or IRA. You select a year that's closest to when you believe you'll retire, such as Target Date Fund 2055. Usually the funds are offered in five-year increments, so choose the closest approximate year. The fund's managers will then automatically invest you in a primarily aggressive portfolio now and then rebalance it to be a more conservative portfolio by the time you plan to retire.

INDIVIDUAL RETIREMENT ARRANGEMENT/ACCOUNT (IRA): IRAs are another way to save up for retirement by investing in stocks and bonds or by leaving money in cash reserves. There are tax advantages to putting money into an IRA, which differ depending on the kind you use. Two of the most common IRAs are traditional or Roth, just like with a 401(k) or 403(b).

- TRADITIONAL: Investing with pre-tax dollars up to the annual limit. You have the potential to lower your taxable liability today.
- ROTH: Investing with post-tax dollars up to the annual limit. The Roth IRA doesn't afford you a tax advantage today, but you do get to withdraw the money tax-free in retirement.

If you're under fifty-nine and a half, you can't withdraw the funds in your IRA without paying a tax penalty. There are some loopholes to this rule. For example, Roth IRAs provide more flexibility for penalty-free withdrawals before retirement age because you've already been taxed on your contributions. Also, when you buy your first home, you may be allowed to raid some of your IRA without triggering a tax penalty. But please don't make any rash decisions about early distributions from a retirement plan before speaking to a tax professional and understanding all the implications.

The IRS does impose limits on how much a person can contribute at what age. In 2018, for example, those under fifty could contribute up to $5,500, and those aged fifty and older could contribute $6,500. Your tax deduction for contributing to a traditional IRA may be limited depending on your income and whether you or a spouse is eligible for a workplace retirement plan. Your eligibility to contribute to a Roth IRA can be limited and even phased out based on your modified adjusted gross income (MAGI), which you will find out when filing your taxes.[1]

ROLLOVER: You don't want to leave your retirement savings behind when you leave a job, so the option is something called a rollover. You can, without triggering tax penalties, take your money out of your existing retirement plan at work as long as you're moving into another retirement plan (e.g., a 401(k) with your new employer or an IRA). It is possible to leave a 401(k) in the hands of your old employer, depending on the stipulations of your plan. However, it's often nice to simplify and bundle all your retirement accounts together instead of having a plan with each of your former employers. Companies like Vanguard, Fidelity, Charles Schwab, and Betterment make it pretty painless to roll over your old 401(k)s or IRAs. I found talking on the phone to a real human helpful the first time I had to do a rollover, just to be extra certain I wouldn't screw anything up.

BENEFICIARY: The person who will receive your money in the case of your death. You're usually asked to designate a beneficiary upon opening a retirement account. You can update your beneficiary at any time, and doing so should be on your to-do list right after any major life events like marriage or becoming a parent. Fun fact: beneficiaries can override a will. A professor of mine shared a story once about karma and beneficiaries. His client's ex-husband had cheated on her and divorced her for his mistress. He died unexpectedly, and while he'd updated his will, he'd never bothered to update his beneficiary on many of his investment accounts. So much of his estate actually went to his first wife instead of the mistress.

HEALTH SAVINGS ACCOUNT (HSA): It may seem strange to include an insurance product in the retirement investing chapter, but an HSA offers you both a tax-advantaged savings vehicle and a way to prepare for future medical expenses, even as far out as retirement. Contributions to your HSA lower your taxable liability, then the money grows tax free, and withdrawals used for qualified medical expenses are also tax free.

You aren't required to spend the money within a certain period of time like you are with a flexible spending account (FSA). There are contribution limits depending on your filing status: e.g., in 2018, they were $3,450 for an individual and $6,900 for a family. Unfortunately, you're eligible for an HSA only if you have a high-deductible health plan.

Now for the reason it makes sense to include this term in a retirement investing chapter (other than the fact that you can save for medical expenses in retirement): The money in your HSA can be invested instead of just sitting in a savings account waiting to be used on medical expenses. Your HSA investment options depend entirely on your provider, but generally there are mutual-fund options.

A shout-out to all my fellow self-employed (or side-gigging) readers.

SIMPLIFIED EMPLOYEE PENSION IRA (SEP IRA): Don't get too excited by the word *pension*. We often wax poetic about the glory days of employers offering pension plans, but this is really just a retirement account for small businesses and the self-employed. It works akin to a traditional

IRA: you get a tax deduction for contributions, and your investments grow tax-deferred until you begin to make withdrawals in retirement. In terms of earning potential, a SEP IRA can trump a traditional IRA because the contribution limits are (potentially) much higher.

In 2018, you can contribute the lesser of 25 percent of your compensation* or $55,000—or in some cases 20 percent of compensation for sole proprietors. That really blows the $5,500 contribution limit on the IRA out of the water. For simplicity's sake, let's say you earned a net profit of $50,000 in self-employment income in 2018 and contributed 25 percent to your SEP IRA. That's $12,500 instead of getting capped at $5,500 for a traditional or Roth IRA.

You're also allowed to contribute to a SEP IRA with side-hustle income, even if you're contributing to a retirement plan through your full-time employer.

A drawback of the SEP IRA is that if your business grows and you acquire employees, you could be required to contribute the same percentage of income to your employees' SEP IRAs as you take yourself.

SOLO (OR INDIVIDUAL) 401(K): This plan is a good fit for a self-employed person who isn't planning to hire full-time employees. You can set it up for yourself and a spouse. A big perk of the solo 401(k) is that you can contribute as both employee and employer, which, depending on your business income, could mean contributing more than you could for a SEP IRA. In 2018, an employee could contribute up to $18,500, and the employer can contribute up to 25 percent of compensation, with a cap of $55,000.[2] The solo 401(k) can also come as a Roth option.

MAXING OUT (AKA CONTRIBUTION LIMITS): Putting the maximum allowable contribution into your retirement account during the year. In

---

*But it caps your eligible compensation at $275,000.

2018, that was $18,500 for an employee contributing to an employer-sponsored 401(k) or 403(b), or up to 100 percent of your income if you made under $18,000. You can find tax information, including the latest contribution limits, at https://www.irs.gov/retirement-plans.

WHAT HAPPENS WHEN YOU CASH OUT A RETIREMENT ACCOUNT EARLY?

Uncle Sam gets an early payday! I jest, a little bit. Tapping into your retirement accounts early, which is generally defined as taking money out before you turn fifty-nine and a half, can result in your paying a penalty to the IRS. (This penalty, in 2018, was 10 percent in addition to any federal and state taxes you owed.) Plus, you lose out on the gains of compound interest.

There are some particular loopholes about withdrawing money from your retirement accounts without triggering penalties—as mentioned earlier, the Roth accounts give you the most flexibility because contributions have already been taxed—but frankly, I don't want to share them lest you consider using one! And because rules are always subject to change and I don't want to outline an option that may not exist in a few years. It's generally best to think of your retirement savings as just that: money to be used in retirement.

Considering a 401(k) loan? As long as you pay it back, taking out a loan against your 401(k) won't trigger tax penalties, which is a positive if it's a last resort. The loan terms usually require you to pay the money back within five years, plus interest that's ultimately paid to you. However, please proceed with caution: if you're fired or quit before the loan is repaid, then you'll probably need to pay it back in full within sixty days.

Leaving a job and unsure what to do with your 401(k)? You may be able to leave it in the current account, or you can roll it over into the 401(k) with your new employer or put it into an IRA.

Oh, here's a fun twist. You're required to start taking money out of traditional IRAs and 401(k) or 403(b) plans once you turn seventy and a half. This is called *required minimum distributions*. Uncle Sam wants to get his cut of your tax-deferred money, so the government requires you to start taking distributions.

THE CASE FOR INVESTING IN MORE THAN YOUR RETIREMENT ACCOUNTS

I once received an email from a Millennial woman named Jessica asking if it was really necessary to invest outside her retirement account. Jessica was maxing out her 401(k), which in 2018 meant she was putting $18,500 a year into her employer's retirement plan, and she had $80,000 in an emergency savings fund.

In truly dramatic fashion, I nearly did a spit take when I read that number.

Eighty thousand dollars is a huge emergency savings fund for most twenty-somethings. Nine months of living expenses is at the high end of what financial experts recommend for an emergency fund, and something told me Jessica didn't need nearly $9,000 a month in case of an emergency. So, I opened up a dialogue to find out why she felt the need for such a high buffer; or if she was saving for a major purchase, like a down payment on a home; or if, as I suspected, she just didn't know what else to do with that money.

Yup, my smell test on Millennial financial behaviors proved correct. Jessica's parents only ever invested in their retirement accounts, and she had no model for why and how she should be putting her money in any investments other than a 401(k) or an IRA.

Jessica's high savings rate and significant emergency fund aren't common for your typical Millennial or, really, any generation, considering that more than half of Americans can't come up with $400 in an emergency.[3] But Jessica's confusion and even concern about investing outside of a retirement account is quite common. I'd argue that plenty of people who do contribute to a 401(k) or 403(b) through work still don't consider themselves investors. I've had many a conversation with a friend that goes something like this:

FRIEND: I don't invest.
ME: Do you have a 401(k) at work?
FRIEND: Yeah.
ME: Do you contribute to it?
FRIEND: Yeah.
ME: Then you're investing, unless it's sitting in cash.

Now that you're starting to think of yourself as an investor, even if it's just in an IRA or 401(k), let's talk about *why* you need to invest outside your retirement accounts. Not to mention that you'll have trouble gaining easy, tax-free access to that retirement money before age fifty-nine and a half.

Goal Setting: Because You Probably Have Things You Want to Do Before Retirement

Saving for retirement is important, but it's an incredibly long-term financial goal that's decades away for most Millennials. You're going to have other major financial goals between now and retirement age, which is why you absolutely need to invest outside your retirement accounts.

Because It's Hard to Save Your Way to Your Goals

"Your money, when you invest it, is doing some of the lifting," explains Jill Schlesinger, CFP®, CBS News business analyst and author of *The Dumb Things Smart People Do with Their Money*.

Trying to save your way to your financial goals will require you to have a significantly higher savings rate than if you invested as well. Just take retirement for example:

Lillian wants to have $1.5 million saved by age seventy in order to comfortably retire. She's currently twenty-five years old and puts $250 out of each biweekly paycheck (i.e., $500 per month) into her 401(k). Assuming an average 7 percent return, Lillian will have more than $1.7 million by the time she reaches her retirement age of seventy.

If Lillian decided to just put $500 a month into a savings account for forty-five years, she'd only have a little over $270,000, especially if it's in a measly 0.01 percent APY savings account. Even if she put that money in a savings account earning 1.00 percent APY, she'd only have about $341,000.

As Schlesinger said, investing allows your money to do some of the heavy lifting.

GOAL SETTING

Investing needs to be coupled with goal setting. After all, knowing your time horizon is part of how you build your portfolio. "I tell my clients all the time, 'I don't care what you spend your money on. I care what your goals are,'" says Douglas Boneparth.

When it comes to your goals, Boneparth recommends that you consider three things: identification, quantification, and prioritization.

Here's how that looks in your life:

1. Identification: What are my financial goals in the next year, three years, five years, ten years, and so on?
2. Quantification: How much money will I need to meet each one of those goals individually?
3. Prioritization: Which goal am I going to focus on first?

Keep in mind: just because you're prioritizing one goal doesn't mean you stop funding your other goals. Paying off student loan debt aggressively doesn't mean you press Pause on funding your 401(k) enough to get the employer match.

Once you identify, quantify, and prioritize your goals, it becomes much easier to put an investing strategy in place. Some financial goals won't require you to invest, such as paying off your student loans or credit card debt. But others, especially medium- (i.e., four to ten years away) and long-term financial goals (ten-plus years away) could seriously benefit from you letting your investments do some of the heavy lifting.

An Example of Goal Setting in Action

When Heather and I found out we were having our daughter, we would've loved to have accelerated our student loan payments, we would've loved to max out our 401(k)s, but top of our priority list was buying a house and handling life logistics: schools, transit, basically getting our life where it needed to be to accommodate the change that was happening. By using the goal system, we were emotionally honest with ourselves about what was important to us. That really puts the "personal" in personal finance.

Heather and I started saving for a home in 2012, and we bought our home [in] August 2016. Take a look at what the market was doing during that time period—it was pretty good. So, you can imagine me as a financial advisor saying, "Man, if I'd just put my money in something as simple as the S&P 500, maybe we could've bought that home a little sooner." Well, what's the flip side? What if there's a correction and things went the other way? I now delayed a goal that needed to happen. There was a kid on the way! The flip side would've been Heather would've removed limbs from my body had I told her we're unable to close on the house because the money we were saving for it went down 20 percent. Imagine if it were 2008. It would've gone down 40 or 50 percent. So, it's a very real example of why, for short-term goals specifically, there is no reward out there appealing enough to outweigh the risk of not accomplishing the goal within the time frame you need. Buying that home a month earlier, because I invested the money, wouldn't have helped my life. But what would've really hurt my life was not being able to close on the home when I really needed to.

—*Douglas A. Boneparth*

WHEN SHOULD YOU BE INVESTING FOR YOUR GOALS?

The next logical question is "Should I invest my savings for short- or medium-term goals?" Here's the truthful but potentially infuriating answer: it depends.

There is always a risk when it comes to investing because the market is going to go down at some point during your time as an investor. Your need to liquidate an investment could coincide with a downturn in the market, which means you either won't get as much bang for your buck or you'll lose money. So, yeah, I get why you could be hesitant to invest for your goals. Saving it just sounds so much safer.

And for short-term goals, I agree with that sentiment. Cash or cash equivalents help mitigate any risk, particularly if your short-term goal isn't a flexible one. Jill Schlesinger advises a one-year rule (two years if you're risk averse). "You're going to business school and planning to write the check or [you're] making a down payment on a house or you need a car," she says. "None of that money can be at risk if you need it within a year."

My husband and I started saving for our honeymoon eighteen months before we planned to take the trip. We had a hard deadline of when we'd need that money, so I wasn't going to invest it in the stock market, because we weren't going to push back the trip if the market tumbled and we needed to wait for it to rebound.

The way in which you'd invest for your medium-term goals depends on your time horizon and on how flexible that deadline can be, and your risk tolerance. A medium-term goal with a deadline of a decade away is one for which you could take some risk early on by investing in stocks and then adjusting your portfolio from moderately aggressive to more conservative—think either bonds and cash or all cash—as your deadline to liquidate and use those funds to make your purchase grows closer.

But if your medium-term goal has a deadline of three years away, and you absolutely must have that money in three years, with no wiggle room to push it back if the market is going through a correction or recession, then it's probably not worth the risk.

SHOULD YOU MAX OUT RETIREMENT ACCOUNTS BEFORE INVESTING IN ANYTHING ELSE?

"Maxing out" a retirement account simply means contributing the maximum allowable contribution. In a perfect world, you should be able to max out your 401(k) with ease and then move on to investing in taxable accounts. Retirement accounts are tax-deferred, so I'll refer to nonretirement investments as "taxable accounts."

"From a sheer growth-of-money perspective, all else being equal, maxing out retirement accounts will be more beneficial due to that fact that you're either saving taxes on the front end, through the pre-tax contributions, or saving taxes on the back end, via Roth, by taking money out tax free," says Boneparth. "If there aren't any other goals or personal preferences and you just want to grow money in the best way possible, there is your answer."

Again, that's in a perfect world. But let's face it, being able to put aside $18,500* into a retirement account is wishful thinking for many, if not most people of all generations.

Saving more than $1,500 per month in your retirement account in order to max it out is a great "reach goal," but before you let it stress you out, reflect on how much you actually think you'll need to live a comfortable life in retirement. Now, there are a lot of variables at play (e.g., inflation, whether your home is paid off, health care, the size of your family), so it can be difficult to know how much you'll need in thirty or forty years. Despite these factors, you can probably come up with an educated

---

*In 2018, $18,500 was the maximum amount you could contribute to a 401(k) or 403(b). For information on current limits, visit www.IRS.gov/retirement-plans.

guess based on your current lifestyle, factoring in paying down debts or adding children.

The Multiply by 25 Rule is a calculation based on the assumption that your retirement will last thirty years and that you're using the 4 Percent Rule. The 4 Percent Rule is a commonly used rule of thumb for a safe withdrawal rate that comes from the 1998 Trinity study,[4] which basically states that if you withdraw 4 percent or less of your portfolio per year and have an appropriate mix of stocks and bonds for your current risk tolerance and phase of life, then your money should last you at least thirty years. You can apply the Multiply by 25 Rule to the amount you think you'll need in retirement in order to determine how much you have to save today.

Some experts prefer people act even more conservatively than the 4 Percent Rule allows and use a 2 or 3 percent annual withdrawal rate, to ensure they won't outlive their nest eggs. Honestly, it's always better to err on the side of caution when it comes to ensuring you won't outlive your money, but I digress.

The Multiply by 25 Rule in Action

Lauren and Dan are currently both twenty-eight and want to retire at age sixty-five. Lauren runs the numbers and decides that she and her husband could comfortably live on $50,000 a year in retirement. Their home would be paid off, any children they plan to have would have graduated college and (hopefully) left home, and neither one of them currently has any sort of chronic medical ailment.

$$(\$50,000 \times 25 = 1,250,000)$$

Lauren and Dan would need $1,250,000 saved in retirement. Now it's time to do the backward planning to determine how much they'll need to save today in order to reach that goal.

Simple situation: Lauren and Dan can each put $500 per month into retirement savings, for a total of $1,000 a month. Assuming a 6 percent annual return over the thirty-seven years they're saving until retirement, that would result in just over $1.5 million saved. That's $300,000 more than they calculated needing, which provides a healthy buffer. Putting $400 each (or $800) away for thirty-seven years would result in their reaching their goal of $1.2 million.

More realistic situation: Lauren has already saved $6,000 in her employer-matched 401(k), which she first got access to at age twenty-five. She receives a 3 percent match on her $45,000 salary. That means her employer contributes $1,350 annually, or $112.50 per month. Lauren contributes 10 percent herself, so she's putting $4,500 a year into her 401(k), or $375 a month. Between Lauren's contribution and her employer's, that's $487.50 a month.

Dan's employer doesn't offer a retirement plan, so he's proactively contributing to a Roth IRA. He's currently contributing $4,000 a year ($333 a month). Assuming the average 6 percent interest rate over the thirty-seven-year period, he and Lauren will have $1.3 million at age sixty-five.

Notably, I've ignored Social Security income in this example and the fact that they'd both receive raises over the years and probably also switch jobs, but you can certainly include all those factors into your own calculations. Have access to a health savings account? Don't forget to factor that in to your retirement planning. Those are super-helpful when it comes to saving tax-deferred money for future medical expenses!

Another factor to consider when deciding whether to max out your retirement accounts: your medium-term goals.

"Here comes personal preferences: if you think you need that money for something else, like you want to buy a house at some point or you plan to make an investment in your business, maybe having accessibility makes sense," says Boneparth.

Investing in a taxable account affords you flexibility. You aren't required to wait until you're fifty-nine and a half to start taking money out without facing a penalty or jumping through hoops. You also aren't required to withdraw your money at any point from a taxable account, as you are with many retirement accounts. Does it make sense for you to lock up all your money for life after age fifty-nine and a half instead of investing it for more medium-term goals?

Now, it is possible to pull money out of your retirement accounts early and, in some cases, without a tax penalty, but as a general rule, just leave your retirement money alone until retirement arrives.

CHECKLIST FOR MAKING SURE YOU'RE READY TO INVEST OUTSIDE OF YOUR RETIREMENT ACCOUNTS

❑ You don't have any high-interest-rate debt.

❑ You've already fully funded your emergency savings with a minimum of three months' worth of living expenses.

❑ You're either maxing out your 401(k) or other retirement savings vehicles already or you have a pre-retirement short- or medium-term financial goal for which you're investing.

❑ You're maxing out your health savings account, if you have access to one.

Chapter 5

Should I Invest When I Have Student Loans?

WHEN PEACH AND I got married in 2018, it meant, in part, the merging of our financial lives. It also represented the first time I would truly have to contend with the student loan debt burden. I'd been fortunate enough to graduate college debt free through a combination of parental support and picking the school where I received the biggest scholarship package.

Fortunately, Peach's debt came as no surprise to me. We'd gotten financially naked with each other long before marriage. But once rings went on fingers, his debt suddenly became a new force in my life. I'd been aggressively saving and investing since my early twenties, and now I wondered if that made the most sense for us as a couple. Perhaps we should funnel our financial resources toward getting debt free as quickly as possible instead.

I've always been debt averse, so the idea of allowing tens of thousands of dollars to weigh down our marital ledger pained me.

We started discussing our options. We could put some of the savings I'd brought into the marriage toward paying off the debt quickly. I could press Pause on investing outside of retirement and put that extra money toward paying off the debt. Peach had only been investing for retirement and otherwise put his money toward his student loans and other short-term goals. Or we could keep paying more than the minimum amount due on his student loans, so the debt would be paid off moderately quickly, and still keep investing, too.

After running the numbers, we decided to use some of our savings to immediately pay off one loan that carried a 7.75 percent interest rate. Instead of depleting a lot of our cash reserves or selling investments, we elected to pay down the remaining loans less aggressively, because of their interest rates. Upon doing the math, it made more sense to have some funds available to keep investing instead of exclusively focusing on debt repayment and pressing Pause on investing.

This plan meant I would need to push back against my psychological desire to be debt free ASAP, but it also was the best decision for our financial health as a couple.

WHETHER TO INVEST while you're paying off student loans is a fiercely debated topic in the personal finance world. It's about half a step below the "Should you be allowed to splurge on nonessentials when you have debt?" debate. (I vote yes, with moderation.)

Truthfully, the answer is simple: yes, you should be investing when you have student loans.

You'll need to buckle up for some actual number crunching in this chapter. It's the only way to make a compelling case for why it's in your best interest to start investing before paying off student loans.

STEP ONE: DO THE MATH ON YOUR INTEREST RATES

There's a significant difference between investing when you're carrying student loan debt and investing when you have credit card debt, also referred to as consumer debt. Your credit card debts probably carry annual percentage rates (or APRs) of 15 to 30 percent. You're not likely to see average returns like that on all your investments from the market in a year and certainly not on average over a longer period of time. Therefore, it doesn't make sense for you to focus on investing when you have a debt accruing 15 to 30 percent in interest, because even with strong market returns, you'd still be losing money.

I'll break it down with actual numbers.

Paying Off Credit Card Debt vs. Investing

Let's say you invested $3,000 in an S&P 500 index fund, and it earned an 8 percent return for two years. Great! You've earned $499.20 by simply investing. But at the same time, you were carrying $3,000 in credit card debt at a 22 percent APR and paying the minimum $120 a month. It would take you thirty-four months to pay off the credit card debt and would cost you over $1,000 in interest. You may have earned $499.20 by having $3,000 invested in the market, but the $499.20 you earned investing minus the $1,000 you paid in interest on your credit card debt means you really lost over $500 by not redirecting that money toward paying off consumer debt.

You might be thinking to yourself, "Wait! You just told me I should still be investing if I have debt." That's because student loans and credit cards aren't the same. So, before you freak out and stop contributing to your retirement accounts and start throwing every spare penny toward student loans, let's consider a similar scenario with student loans.

Paying Off Student Loan Debt vs. Investing

Let's say Olivia took out $11,000 in direct unsubsidized federal student loans carrying an interest rate of 4.66 percent.[1] She also has $7,000 in student loans from Discover with a fixed rate of 6.50 percent. Between the two, her average interest rate is 5.58 percent. Olivia is required to pay $196 a month, but pays an extra $54 to make the payment an even $250. So, to review, that's:

- $18,000 in student loans
- Average interest rate: 5.58 percent
- Monthly payment required: $196
- Olivia pays: $250

To get a better sense of Olivia's monthly budget, you should know that she contributes to her employer-sponsored 401(k) program, puts money into savings, pays all her bills, and puts money aside for her general monthly living expenses, including entertainment. After all that, she still has an extra $200 a month. Her financial oxygen mask is fully affixed.

Even though Olivia is paying above the minimum due on her student loans, she isn't fixated on aggressively paying off her debt. She wants to buy a house in about ten years, so she's interested in making her money do some of the work, so she decides to put the extra $200 a month into an S&P 500 index fund.

Now we're going to fast-forward eight years. Olivia's paid off her student loans. The extra $54 a month in payments helped her reduce her loan repayment period from ten years to just over seven. She forked over $3,969 in interest on top of the $18,000 principal balance owed.[2]

If Olivia had put the extra $200 a month toward her student loans instead of investing it, she would've paid off her debt in just under four years and spent approximately $2,000 on interest instead of the $3,969 she paid. That's nearly $2,000 she could've saved on interest, not to mention being done with payments in about half the time. She'd also have $450 freed up per month to put toward saving for her down payment.

If Olivia chose not to pay off the debt quickly and invested instead, after eight years of consistently putting $200 a month into an S&P 500 index fund, she invested a total of $19,200, which earned an average 7 percent return over those eight years. Her grand total in the account is currently $24,623.53. That's a return of $5,423.53. Not a bad return, but there are three things to consider. First, Olivia paid nearly $2,000 more in interest by not paying off her student loans aggressively with her extra $200. After subtracting that $2,000, her return is still up about $3,500 from investing, but she probably wouldn't have invested for all eight years because ... Second, if Olivia wanted to stay on the time horizon of buying a home in ten years, then she would've needed to move her investments to a more conservative investment around year 5. That would've resulted in a portfolio of

$13,800 and a return of only $1,800. Third, market returns may not have been average. She might've caught a bear market and had really low returns for five years.

So, should Olivia be investing this way while dealing with student loan debt?

"Do you have an employer plan with a match? If the answer is yes, then definitely use your plan up to the match and use the rest of your money to pay down the loans," advises Jill Schlesinger, CFP®, CBS News business analyst and author of *The Dumb Things Smart People Do with Their Money*. "If you want to get into the habit of saving for retirement, yeah, put 5 percent in, but don't go crazy, because we do have to pay off your debt. And the debt's not going away on its own. I'm someone who has lived through so many crashes and so many horrible events that I'm really risk averse. So, in my mind, I'd much prefer to take a sure thing of paying down a 6 or 5 percent note that's really not going to do much for me. Yes, it depends, and yes, there are different folks that will be able to earn more, but for most of us, it's just a balancing act."

But What If Your Situation Is Nothing Like Olivia's?

Olivia is a fortunate, fictional character. She has enough money month to month that her bills are paid, she's got living expenses on lock, she has money going toward financial goals, *and* she can still put $200 toward investing. Uh, eye roll please. Who lives like that?

I get it. It's rare to have a situation like Olivia's. You may just be at the point of feeling in control from month to month and feel good about having a spare $25 a month to invest. That's okay. For one thing, your situation is going to change. Debts will start to reduce. You'll eventually start earning more. You will get to a point where you have discretionary income to put toward investing.

In the meantime, you should at least be investing in your employer-matched retirement account as a means of investing while you're paying off student loans.

Consider Why You're Investing While in Debt

You must never forget the importance of goal setting, time horizon, risk tolerance, and asset allocation. These factors are particularly critical when it comes to deciding if it makes sense to invest while paying off debt. When will you need this money? If you're on a medium-term time horizon of under ten years, does it make sense to put risk on the money, or would that money be better served getting you to debt freedom? Can you emotionally handle seeing your investments drop during this period?

Have You Considered Refinancing?

Refinancing is the act of taking out a new loan to pay off an existing one. It sounds sketchy as hell when you put it that way, but it can be a valuable tool. Let's say Toru is carrying $20,000 in student loan debt at a 6.5 percent rate on a ten-year term. He applies and gets approved for refinancing at a 4.5 percent rate on a ten-year term. Not only can he now pay less in monthly payments, but he will also save more than $2,000 in interest over the life of the loan.

Refinancing your student loan debt to get a lower interest rate enables you to attack the debt more efficiently and also free up funds for other financial goals. Unfortunately, it's easier said than done. You may find that it's harder for you to get approved than you expected or that the interest rate you're offered isn't as competitive as you'd hoped. Refinance companies don't readily share underwriting criteria for approval, but the ideal candidates have strong credit scores (700+), have completed their degrees, have been employed for at least a year, have never missed a student loan payment, and it doesn't hurt if they have a healthy salary.

Douglas Boneparth and his wife, Heather, refinanced their loans from Heather's law school degree and Douglas's MBA. "Heather and I refinanced more than $300,000 from the federal rates of 6.8 percent to 7.9 percent down to 2.95 percent. We went from a thirty-year repayment plan down to fifteen years for $200 less a month. It's the Holy Grail of refinance situations. It allowed us to not only free up cash flow each month, but also cut the term in half and pay tens to hundreds of thousands of dollars less in interest over the life of the loan."

The downsides of refinancing: You turn federal loans into private loans, which means you lose eligibility for any federal programs, such as debt forgiveness or income-driven repayment plans. Also, with private loans, deferment and forbearance, which allow you to temporarily stop making payments on your student loans due to hardship circumstances, aren't as easy to come by compared to the options for federal student loans. Student loan refinance companies include: SoFi, earnest, Laurel Road, and CommonBond.

When Do the Experts Say It's Okay To Be Investing While in Debt?

There is not one specific interest rate upon which the entire industry agrees, except that if it's high—especially in double digits—you should focus on paying off your debt first.

"If you have a very low interest rate on that student loan debt and it's less than 5 percent or less than 4 percent, you might consider investing into the market while you're also paying that off," says Julie Virta, senior financial advisor with Vanguard Personal Advisor Services. "We look at it from a financial situation. If you expect your portfolio to earn 6 to 8 percent, and your student loan debt is at 3, 4, or 5 percent, maybe, you're better off investing your dollars."

Virta does advise considering the climate in which you're investing. After the Great Recession the stock market experienced a bull run from 2009 through 2018, but analysts and experts have been anticipating a market correction and less aggressive returns in the coming years. No one has a crystal ball, of course, but always do your research about recent returns before deciding to invest while paying off debt.

"We tend to say: anything above 7 percent, pay it off," says Sallie Krawcheck, CEO of Ellevest. "For context, the stock market on average, since the 1920s, returns about 9.5 percent annually. Now, some years it's been a lot better and some years it's been a lot worse, but that's the annual average. We believe a well-diversified investment portfolio should return about 6 percent annually. That gives you a guidepost."

"People should have an emergency fund and no high-interest debt before they start investing," says Alex Benke, vice president of Financial Advice and Planning for Betterment. "You could have mortgage debt and student loan debt, depending on the rate, before investing. Five percent is what we [at Betterment] use as cut-off on student loan debt."[3]

That being said, Benke also advises to still take advantage of an employer-matched retirement plan, even if your student loan debt is above 5 percent. The 5 percent rule refers to general investing in taxable accounts.

In fact, all the experts I interviewed for this book agree that when you have the option to invest in an employer-matched retirement account, you should do it.

STEP TWO: AT LEAST INVEST IN RETIREMENT VEHICLES

"With this generation and the next generation that's coming out of school with so much debt, if you wait to invest until you pay off the debt, you're at a real disadvantage," admits Jennifer Barrett, chief education officer for Acorns.

As discussed in chapter 4, sticking money into a 401(k) or 403(b) is investing. Well, it's investing as long as the money isn't just sitting in the account in cash. Even when you're carrying student loan debt, it's important to think long-term about retirement decades from now.

"It's not either/or," advises Colleen Jaconetti , CFP®, senior investment analyst for Vanguard Investment Strategy Group, who acknowledges that people love to come up with a million reasons not to save. "It's the difference between what you are paying on the debt relative to what you could make in the market. And be realistic about what you could make in the market. Certainly, if it's high credit card debt, like 25 percent, pay that off first. If we're talking student loans at 2, 3, 4 percent relative to what you could make in the market, definitely consider investing at least up to the match. Get the match on your 401(k) before paying extra on the student loans."

To give an example, let's meet Erica:

Erica is paying off $30,000 in student loan debt at 4.66 percent with a monthly payment of $313 on a ten-year plan. Putting money into her employer-matched 401(k) is not a top priority right now. She's earning $55,000 a year, and her company will match her contributions up to 4 percent. In real talk, that means if Erica puts $2,200 a year in her 401(k)—which is 4 percent of $55,000—then her employer will also put $2,200 a year in to match her contribution. That's roughly $84.60 out of each of her biweekly paychecks, a sum that is also about half Erica's monthly student loan payment. Erica would rather put that extra money toward paying off her debt quickly.

But here's the issue: Erica's leaving $2,200 a year in free money on the table. She can only get the employer match if she contributes to her 401(k) herself.

Erica is a Millennial, so the odds of her staying with this company for a decade may be slim, but let's just say she does. For ten years, she picks up an additional $2,200 from her employer simply by contributing to her 401(k). That's an extra $22,000 before market returns. And come on, obviously Erica will get promotions and raises, so it will definitely be even more than $22,000 over a ten-year period.

Now let's go back to the student loan debt. In the decade it would take Erica to pay off the $30,000 at 4.66 percent with a monthly payment of $313, she would pay about $7,590 in interest. That means, in total, her student loans cost her $37,590.

If Erica put an extra $169.20 a month toward her student loans instead of her 401(k), she would pay off her loans in six years (about four years faster) and save about $3,200 in interest. That sounds great, except the math doesn't actually add up.

In those six years, she could've put that $2,200 a year into her

401(k) and received an additional $2,200 from her employer, for a total of $4,400 a year.

What would Erica's 401(k) look like if she been putting in $2,200 and getting matched for six years, with an average annual return of 7 percent? She'd have nearly $32,000 in her retirement savings. That's almost the full amount of her student loan. If she lets that money continue to grow while she contributes that $4,400 a year to it, in four more years, she'll have amassed about $61,000. That's $30,800 *more* than her *entire* student loan debt. It's a hell of a lot more than the $3,200 she saved in interest by paying off her student loan debt more quickly.

"What is it costing you to service these loans, and what opportunity costs are you missing out on by not investing?" asks Jaconetti.

Erica, do the right thing. Invest in your 401(k).

I'm Self-Employed, with No Employer Match— Should I Still Prioritize Retirement?

Not everyone has the luxury of a 401(k) option. I'm a self-employed Millennial, too, so I get the struggle of deciding between funding today's financial goals versus putting money into an account that essentially locks away your money until you're fifty-nine and a half. Not to mention that we don't get the bonus of an employer match.

Being self-employed with unpredictable income can make it difficult to balance financial priorities. But even though you're dealing with student loan debt, it is still wise to invest for retirement. You want the advantage of compound interest working for you for the extra decade of your life, especially if it's going to take you ten to twenty years to pay off your student loans.

I Can't Afford to Put Much into Retirement, Yet

Sure, the Erica example is simplistic and rather cut-and-dried. She's making a decent salary, and her student loan payments seem manageable. I get that it's certainly not the typical situation for many Millennials who don't feel as if they've gotten their financial lives together and put that financial oxygen mask on. You may feel as if every single penny is spoken for in your paycheck and that putting enough away to get your employer match is simply not doable.

"So, they say you should target 12 to 15 percent of your income toward retirement," says Maria Bruno, CFP®, a senior investment analyst for Vanguard Investment Strategy Group. "Well, if I have that conversation with someone who's in their twenties, they look at me like I'm crazy. I lose all credibility. So what I would suggest would be to save at least up to the company match, if you have that opportunity, and then do a 1 percent increase every year. And maybe you're saving 5 percent plus a 3 percent company match. You're at 8 percent out of the gate. You do a 1 percent automatic increase every year. If you're twenty-five when you start, by the year you hit thirty, you're pretty much within that ballpark in a very comfortable way."

Bruno's strategy of increasing in small increments over time is also a way to work up to getting your employer match in the first place. Start by putting just 1 percent in your 401(k). After six months, kick it up half a percent or all the way to 2 percent. Then keep increasing it every six months until you've worked up to getting the employer match. When it's just 1 percent at a time, you honestly barely notice the difference in your paycheck—especially if you're lowering your taxable income.

If Nothing Else, Consider the Tax Benefits

Math-heavy arguments showing why compound interest is your best friend and why you should invest early and often in order to take advantage of it, even with student loans, really might not get you going the way they do for me. That's okay. Here's another argument for why you should at least contribute to your retirement account even while carrying student loans: taxes.

"I think you want to make retirement investing a priority because there's tax benefits to doing so, even if you don't get a company match, for instance. Or if you don't participate in a 401(k) through your employer, there's individual retirement accounts or other vehicles that you can use that have tax benefits," says Bruno. "And that starts the tax-free or the tax-deferred clock ticking right away. So you want to make that a priority. But it's okay to do that and balance debt as well."

Contributing to a tax-deferred account such as a traditional 401(k) or IRA means you lower your taxable income today. When you take the money out in retirement, you'll have to pay taxes on it. A Roth account means you don't get the tax perk today, but you will in retirement. You put money into a Roth account after paying taxes, but you get to take the money out in retirement tax free.

That said, there is one completely valid reason you may want to hit Pause on making retirement contributions: your debt tolerance.

WHAT'S YOUR DEBT TOLERANCE?

"I really regret paying my debt off quickly," said no one ever, because debt sucks with a capital S-U-C-K-S.

I can give you all the mathematical reasons as to why you need to be investing. I can make impassioned pleas about compound interest and the value of having time on your side and how it's incredibly difficult to make up ground ten years later, even if you double down on your contributions. But for all my eloquent arguments, your gut might just say, "No, I'm completely uncomfortable with debt and it needs to be gone at any cost."

That's okay. You may have a massive case of debt aversion. I'm one of you, too. The idea of hanging on to debt for a decade, even when it mathematically makes sense to do so, gives me a low-grade case of nausea. It's something I've been working on getting over while dealing with my husband's loans. We're attacking his debt with a three-pronged approach of moderately aggressive repayment, prioritizing retirement savings, and mixing in some investing.

Ultimately, you do have to decide what the right decision is for you emotionally and not just financially. Just do the future you a favor and consider the financial side a little bit. At least put some money into retirement savings, please. Okay, I'll get off my soapbox now.

"You're the circus unicyclist spinning plates with a kazoo in your mouth," jokes Schlesinger. "That's what your financial life is when you're in your twenties and thirties. And you've got to balance a lot of different needs. So just be reasonable and know yourself. If that debt is keeping you up at night, even if it's just 2 percent, then pay the frickin' thing off!"

CHECKLIST FOR INVESTING WHILE YOU HAVE STUDENT LOAN DEBT

❑ Get the employer match!

- If it hasn't been made abundantly clear by now, you shouldn't aggressively pay off debt in lieu of putting money away for retirement, especially when an employer match is involved.

❑ Crunch the numbers on your interest rates.

- Are the interest rates on your student loans above 5 percent? Then it probably makes sense to prioritize the debt payoff over investing outside of retirement accounts.

❑ Know your risk tolerance.

- Can you emotionally handle investing while in debt or will a dip in your portfolio trigger you to sell when the market is low?

❑ Embrace your emotional relationship to debt.

- If you legitimately can't sleep at night because of your debt, then it's okay to make paying it off a priority. But please, please, please, at least get an employer match or put some money away in a retirement account if you're self-employed!

Chapter 6

I Want to Put Money in the Market— How Do I Start?

THERE I WAS, two years out of college, earning a whopping $37,500 a year at my job and bringing in a few extra grand a year in small writing jobs and babysitting. Despite living in one of the most expensive cities in the United States, I officially had my financial oxygen mask on. A fully funded emergency savings and no debt made me feel empowered to start investing outside the 401(k) I had at work. Except I had no clue what to do, and in retrospect, I wouldn't have done what I did next.

I made the entirely un-Millennial move of calling up my bank.

Now, I will say that I loved, and still love, this particular bank. It has great customer service, which was what inspired my phone call. I didn't know what I was doing, so speaking to a real person helped reduce my anxiety about screwing up. I hadn't done any research about fees or set goals or determined my time horizon or risk tolerance.

Carol answered my call and assured me she could help me set up my first investment. To do this, she asked some basic questions to determine how I should be investing.

She asked me when I thought I'd want the money. "Uh, I don't know. Maybe for a house in ten years?"

She asked how much money I had to invest. "I've saved up $2,000 to invest."

She inquired about my risk tolerance. "Hmm, I don't mind taking some risk, I guess."

As you can sense, my responses were not particularly well thought out. But thirty minutes or so later, I had my first taxable account set up: a mutual fund that, unbeknownst to me at the time, came with rather high fees.

I basked in the self-important glow of being twenty-four years old with a 401(k) *and* a mutual fund.

Silly, Erin. You still sort of screwed up.

While I guess it's good that I took a step toward investing, albeit an uninformed one, and while I felt a smidgen of dignity in trying to be a grown-up and not calling my dad this time for advice (even though I probably should've), this is not the method you should use.

OKAY, BUT SERIOUSLY, THEN—HOW DO I GET STARTED?

"I want to invest, but how do I start?" is probably the most common investing question I receive. It's completely justified because it isn't a straightforward process. We aren't taught how to do it in school, googling the question yields an overwhelming amount of options that rarely actually show you how to open an account, and your parents may have never invested, either. Our go-to resources have failed!

This chapter will give you an overview of how to open a brokerage account and some of the options available to you. This will be focused more on investing in mutual, index, or exchange-traded funds. There is some overlap with what you need if you plan to do individual stock picking, too, but that topic is addressed in chapter 7.

Because this book is in print, which means I can't update it like I could a blog post, there will be certain points at which I'm a bit vague. I don't want to put a detail or direction in print that will be irrelevant in a few years or maybe even by the time this book is in your hands! In these moments of vagueness, I'll do my best to direct you to places where you can find up-to-date information.

WHAT YOU NEED TO OPEN A BROKERAGE ACCOUNT

Before you even walk into a brokerage firm or, more realistically, go to its website, here are the pieces of information you'll need for a smooth process:

- Personal information: You'll be asked for your name, address, email address, telephone number, date of birth, employment status, and occupation. The brokerage will also want to know if you're employed by a brokerage firm.[1]
- Social Security number or other tax identification number: The money you earn investing is subject to taxation, so the brokerage firm has to be able to report that income to the IRS. This number is also used to verify your identity.
- Government-issued identification: Your driver's license, passport, or similar identification cards will be required. The brokerage firm needs this to comply with the USA PATRIOT Act of 2001 and to further verify your identity.[2]
- Financial information: You will be asked about your annual income, net worth, and investment objectives. Brokerages and advisors need this information in order to comply with state and US laws as well as rules from regulatory bodies like the Securities and Exchange Commission (SEC) and the Financial Industry Regulatory Authority (FINRA). Your broker may also use this information to determine suitable investment recommendations.
- Bank information: You need the routing and account number for the checking account you'll use to fund your new brokerage account.

WHAT YOU SHOULD DECIDE BEFORE YOU BEGIN

You've collected all your personal information and now you're ready to set up your brokerage account. But first you need to know a couple of things:

What Kind of Account You Want to Open

Are you investing for retirement, education (e.g., your child's college education), or for other financial goals? The type of account you open will depend on the reason you're investing in the first place. In this case, let's assume you are investing for a medium- to long-term goal.

Don't be like me and just randomly pick something with little to no forethought. But the one right move I made was talking to someone when I felt I needed help. I advise that you give your investment strategy more thought than I did, but picking up the phone and talking to an advisor at your potential brokerage firm is smart.

How to Fund the Account and How Much to Invest

You could write a check (if you even have a checkbook!) or make a transfer from your bank account. Have your routing and account numbers ready.

You should also have decided how much you want or need to invest. Some funds have a minimum initial investment.

If your investing is retirement related, you might be doing a rollover from a former employer's 401(k). Or you could transfer a brokerage account you already have at another financial institution to fund your new endeavor.

OTHER QUESTIONS YOU MAY BE ASKED
WHILE SETTING UP YOUR ACCOUNT

Here are three other questions you may need to answer when setting up your account:

Would You Like a Cash Account or a Margin Loan Account?

As a rookie, it's best to go with a cash account. A cash account means you'll be paying for the investments you purchase in full. A margin loan means the broker can lend you funds to make the purchase, so you're buying "on margin." Money already in your account works as collateral for the loan. It's simpler not to complicate the process, so choose a cash account.

What Do You Want to Do with Your Dividends?

You will be asked, at some point, what you want to do with the dividends your investment earns (assuming it earns dividends). You could take them in cash each year or you could just reinvest them, using a dividend reinvestment plan, or DRIP).

This isn't a black-and-white situation in which one is completely superior. It comes back to your goals. Why are you investing this money? Are you trying to get some passive income right now or do you want to maximize as much growth as possible for the future, when you plan to sell the stock? Reinvesting is going to be beneficial for long-term growth.

Who Is Your Beneficiary?

The beneficiary is the person who will receive the money in your account upon your death. Please take the few minutes it requires to set up a beneficiary. You usually need the person's full legal name, birth date, address, and Social Security number. Designating a beneficiary helps reduce confusion and tension for your loved ones after your death. Plus, it could help your loved ones avoid probate, in which a court supervises the distribution of your estate.

WHICH BROKERAGE SHOULD I USE?

Okay, you've pulled all the information together that you need to open the account. Now the big question: where should you take your business?

You have many options when it comes to picking a brokerage firm. This may be a disappointment, but I'm not going to tell you which one to pick. I can't! I don't know what best suits your needs. Instead, I'm going to provide you with a way to vet brokerage firms to find one that's the right fit.

"Vet them like a dating partner," says Kelly Lannan at Fidelity Investments. "Is this someone who has my best interest at heart? This is someone whom I might spend the rest of my life working with. As a result, those are pretty high standards."

What Kind of Service Do You Want or Need?

Do you plan to do lots of trading, or will you be a buy-and-hold investor? Do you want to be more hands-on and DIY in your approach, or would you feel more confident if you connected with a human or had an algorithm maximizing your portfolio? These are the factors you need to take into consideration when determining whether a brokerage firm is right for you.

What Are the Minimums for Opening an Account?

Many, but not all, brokerage firms will have minimum initial investments in order to open an account at all or to invest in certain funds. These minimums vary, and therefore can have a huge impact on which institution you pick. Let's say you have $1,500 to get started on your investing journey and you've picked an index fund in which you want to invest. Well, that's going to rule out any brokerage with a minimum investment greater than $1,500 for that fund.

If you're dead set on a certain brokerage firm, but its minimum is too high, then you have a few options:

- Search and see if another comparable fund at the same brokerage has a lower initial investment requirement.
- Start investing at a different brokerage and transfer your funds after you've met the investment minimum at the brokerage you want.

- Keep saving up until you hit the minimum.
- See if the exchange-traded fund (ETF) version is cheaper than the mutual fund version. Sometimes it is!

How Reputable and Well Liked Is the Brokerage?

Honestly, my favorite strategy here is word of mouth. Do any of your friends, cousins, parents, aunts, uncles, or parents of friends invest? If so, ask them which brokerage firm they use, why, and how they like it. Try to crowdsource from more than just one or two people.

Then, take to the internet.

Type in the name of the brokerage firm and "reviews" to get a sense of what people outside your immediate circle think. Be sure to also read about the negative experiences customers shared.

You can also see what Morningstar has to say about specific funds in which you want to invest. This investment research company ranks funds out of five stars, so it's easy to see how your potential investment stacks up.

How Is Its Customer Service?

You don't have to be a current client to take the firm's customer service out for a test drive. Give the brokerage a call. Use the opportunity to see how long you're kept on hold and how you're treated by the customer service representative. You should also check whether email and live chat are options for connecting with customer service. You want to be doing business with an institution that treats you and other customers well.

How Would You Rate Its Website and App?

I'll be honest: a few of the websites out there are not the streamlined experience most Millennials are used to. Hopefully that changes soon, but if a particular kind of user experience on a website or app is important to you, then you should test-drive both before picking a brokerage.

How Hefty Are the Fees?

Always determine what your potential brokerage firm will charge you to be a customer. Does the brokerage charge you a fee for "assets under management" (AUM)? For example, a 2 percent fee on your portfolio of $10,000 means you'll be paying $200 annually, which could be in addition to other trading fees. Are you receiving $200 worth of guidance and value? Later on in this chapter, we'll overview various fees you may experience and how to decode the almighty expense ratio we defined in chapter 2.

Does It Uphold Suitability or Fiduciary Standards?

Perhaps you've decided to pay for investing advice. That's perfectly okay, but you should know what type of advice you're receiving. Is your advisor being held to the suitability standard (i.e., the recommendations are suitable for you) or the fiduciary standard (i.e., the recommendations are in your best interest)? You should also know if and how your broker receives any commissions on products he or she puts in your portfolio.

Okay, Okay—I'll Name Some Names

I know you're still wondering, "BUT WHERE DO I GO?" I hear you, so I'll overview different kinds of brokerages and list some actual options. Please be aware that I'm in no way endorsing these particular options, but simply acknowledging their existence in the space.

Full-Service Brokerage Firms

With a full-service firm, you'll have an advisor helping you build and manage your portfolio, but you'll pay higher fees. This might sound like the better option for a novice investor because an expert is helping you out. The issue: a full-service brokerage may not want to work with you. You often need to be bringing some serious money to the table to have an actively managed portfolio of this nature. This isn't always the case, but there's a reason the stereotype of needing double commas (aka $1 million or more) in order to be taken seriously exists.

Still, with some competition in the marketplace, plenty of firms have much lower asset minimums than $1 million, but the level of guidance and advice you get may vary based on your account balance. You'll need to do your research if you plan to go with a full-service brokerage firm.

Examples of a full-service brokerage firm include: Morgan Stanley, UBS, Edward Jones, and Merrill Lynch. There are also investment banks like J.P. Morgan Private Bank and Wells Fargo that offer investment advice and financial planning services.

Discount Brokerage Firms

With the discount brokerage firm, you'll be taking the DIY approach and therefore will save more in fees. Plenty of both rookie and seasoned investors utilize the DIY approach to investing, including yours truly. There is a lower barrier to entry than with a full-service brokerage, because you only need a little money to get started. Some, but certainly not all, funds at a discount brokerage may have minimum initial investments, often $1,000 to $3,000.

Similar to the full-service brokerages, some discount brokerage firms also offer access to financial advisors, but you usually need to have a certain amount of money invested with the firm in order to unlock that feature. For example, if you have $50,000 in investments, then you gain access to investment professionals for general guidance. If you have $500,000 in investments, then you get to consult with a certified financial planner (CFP) for no additional fee if you have a specific question. Just because you go with a discount brokerage firm doesn't mean you'll be without personalized guidance.

If you don't have the amount of money invested that's required to unlock the personalized advisor features, then you can always call customer service for general help.

Examples of discount brokerages include Vanguard, Fidelity, Charles Schwab, TD Ameritrade, T. Rowe Price, and Ally Invest.

Online Financial Advisors (aka Robo-Advisors)

Robo-advisor is the term often used to refer to digital platforms for investing. Robo-advisors are typically perceived as having little to no human interaction and relying on an algorithm, but that's not entirely correct.

"*Robo-advising*, the term is too narrow," says Alex Benke, CFP®, Betterment's VP for financial advice and planning. "People think of Betterment as a robo-advisor, but we have an offering that involves people, too. We [Betterment] think *online financial advisor* is more accurate. It implies use of technology, but it doesn't pigeonhole in terms of how you're getting that advice."

Robo-advisors or online financial advisors are marketed to Millennials as a digital solution for the often intimidating process of investing. You're asked some questions online and given recommendations on about how to best build your portfolio. They can be quite helpful to a novice investor who wants either a little more hand-holding or to take advantage of other offerings, like frequent rebalancing and tax-loss harvesting. There will be more information about robo-advisors in chapter 9.

One potential downside to the online financial advisor route is paying a higher fee for access to funds you could purchase directly through the discount brokerage firms like Vanguard, Fidelity, and Schwab. However, that fee could be worth the value you're receiving. It's up to you to decide. It should also be noted that some brokerage firms have tried competing with the online financial advisor by adding on a robo option. You should critically evaluate whether those add-ons provide the same value. Some do and some don't.

Examples of online financial advisors include: Betterment, Swell, Personal Capital, Wealthfront, Wealthsimple, and Ellevest.

Apps

Yes, there is most certainly an app for that. Robinhood, Acorns, and Stash are all examples of apps with which you can invest via the touch of a button on your phone. Chapter 8 will overview using apps for investing.

PICKING YOUR INVESTMENTS

Yet again I'll have to disappoint you a bit. I can't give you a definitive answer because I don't know anything about your goals, risk tolerance, or time horizon. But I can tell you this:

First, you'll need to decide if you want to go the actively managed mutual fund route or the passively managed index fund or ETF route. Both are valid, but don't forget that "actively managed" means you'll pay more in fees.

Second, you'll need to reflect on the goal for this money and the kind of risk you want to take. (Refer back to chapter 4 for setting actionable goals.)

Third, you'll need to diversify as you build your portfolio. You don't want to just pick one stock in one sector. Investing in mutual, index, or exchange-traded funds gives you exposure to a variety of sectors and companies, and is a good first step. Examples of funds that do that would be the S&P 500, Total Stock Market, and Total International Stock Market, but notably those are all on the high-risk end of the spectrum. Total Bond Market would be more conservative, while a Balanced Fund offers an approximately 60/40 split on stocks and bonds and is medium on the risk spectrum.

UNDERSTANDING THE FEES

Now it's time to add one more important factor when choosing your brokerage firm and investments: fees. I mentioned earlier that fees need to be a critical part of the decision-making process, so let's do a deep dive into the fees you may encounter and how to decode them.

Expense Ratios 101

You're going to pay fees on your investments. The brokerages aren't nonprofit institutions, and at the bare minimum, they need to cover the administrative costs of running a fund. Even if your app or trading platform says "no fee," that usually means it doesn't take a commission on your trade, but the stock you buy or the ETF or mutual fund does have an expense ratio. In 2016, the average expense ratio across funds was 0.57 percent, according to a Morningstar study of US funds.[3] This cost is generally deducted from the fund's average net assets.

That being said, fees range significantly from modest to hefty. As Colleen Jaconetti, CFP®, a senior investment analyst for Vanguard Investment Strategy Group, mentioned in chapter 4, the more you pay in fees, the more those fees eat away at your growth potential as well as the amount of money you'll have in the future.

Where to Find the Expense Ratio

Expense ratios are (or should be) prominently displayed under the details or facts about the fund. You could download the fund's prospectus and look for it there. Or just go to the brokerage's website, search for the fund, and then hit Control-F and search for "expenses" or "exp ratio" or "expense ratio" to hunt it down.

If you can't easily find this on a brokerage's website, go to Morning star.com and search for the name of the fund. Morningstar analyzes and provides data about the stock market.

But What Does the Expense Ratio Mean?

If, right next to an index fund, it says "0.14 percent expense ratio," what does that mean?

"They're going to charge you $4 for every $1,000 you have invested," says Jaconetti.

What's a Reasonable Expense Ratio?

"I would say at least somewhere below 50 basis points would be reasonable," explains Jaconetti. "It's still a little on the high end relative to what you could be getting, but obviously anything above 50 basis points, I would say is on the higher end."

What the Heck Is a Basis Point?
Pretty much just a fancy way of expressing the expense ratio. A fund charging you 50 basis points charges you 0.50 percent. One basis point = 0.01 percent.

Why an Expense Ratio Might Be on the High Side
The way your fund is managed will impact the expense ratio. Passively managed funds are going to be cheaper than actively managed funds.

Investing in international funds is another reason you may encounter a higher expense ratio. Global diversification (investing in funds outside the US stock market) is part of a balanced portfolio because it spreads out your risk, but it does often result in a higher expense ratio than investing in the US market. For example, you might get 0.26 percent on an international fund compared to 0.14 percent on a US market fund.

What Should I Expect If I'm Paying a Higher Expense Ratio?
"People shrug their shoulders at 1 percent, but we know how that adds up," says Alex Benke, CFP®, Betterment's VP of financial advice and planning. "But at some point, you get down to it and think, 'Yeah, even a quarter of a percent is costing me a bunch of money over time,' so the struggle there is to evaluate the payment for the value that you're getting."

Benke points to the various online financial advisors (aka robo-advisors) and suggests being highly critical about whether the one you plan to use is balancing cost and value. Evaluate if you are receiving value for the cost, or if it's just setting up a portfolio for you without any added benefit. For example: is there tax-loss harvesting, rebalancing, or a streamlined user experience?

"When considering the value you're getting out of something, you want to look at the dollars-and-cents value," says Benke. "Is it squeezing out as much from your money as it can in terms of funds you get put in and taxes it can save you? But also, is it actually making your life easier in terms of the time that you're investing?"

Similarly, Jaconetti recommends thinking about your "why": are the fees for advice or just for the fund or product? "Some people are willing to pay a fee because they think the manager will have outstanding performance going forward," she explains, but she warns you to keep in mind that past performance is not indicative of future performance. Assuming your fund manager does outperform the market, you should still do the math to see if you received a higher return after fees.

Paying for advice is a personal decision, but this could justify a higher expense ratio, especially if it helps you create a tax-advantaged strategy for your investments.

Can I Lower the Expense Ratio?

Investing more is an easy way to reduce an expense ratio. Well, it's "easy" in the sense of being simple, not that you can magically come up with more money to invest.

Slow-and-Steady in Action

When I first started investing, I was woefully ignorant that investing more could lower my expense ratio. I picked a fund with a minimum investment requirement of $3,000 and diligently contributed monthly. The expense ratio was 0.15 percent. A few years later, I made my monthly contribution and received a prompt that I could convert to a new fund and reduce my expense ratio to 0.04 percent. *What?!* Turns out, once my investment hit $10,000, the brokerage offered a reduced expense ratio for the same investment. I converted to the new fund and saved myself 11 basis points, which also meant keeping more in my pocket for future growth.

Other Fees

Not all brokerage firms charge these fees, and fees also vary by fund. You can find more details about fees by downloading its prospectus. A prospectus is a document that overviews the investment to potential and current investors. It's a legal document and required by and filed with the SEC. A prospectus generally includes information about what the company does, its strategy, its financial details, the risk involved, and fees. It should be readily available on any webpage detailing information about the fund. Here are some of the fees you may see on a prospectus. Notably, the expense ratio may be referred to as "management fees" and/or "total annual fund operating expenses" on a prospectus.

ASSETS UNDER MANAGEMENT (AUM): A flat-rate fee is paid to your advisor based on the size of your portfolio (i.e., your assets under management). For example, a 2 percent AUM on your $100,000 portfolio means you're paying $2,000 to your advisor for his or her services.

COMMISSION: Your advisor or broker receives a commission for opening an account on your behalf or selling you particular products. Your advisor isn't necessarily acting in a nefarious manner if he or she receives a commission, but you should be aware if that's the case and ensure the product matches the fiduciary standard and not the suitability standard, because fiduciary ensures it's in your best interest, not just suitable. You don't want a subpar product in your investment portfolio just because your advisor gets a commission off the sale.

TRADING OR TRANSACTION FEE: A commission or trading fee is usually charged when you buy or sell shares of stocks through an ETF or buy individual stocks through your brokerage. A transaction fee may also be charged when you buy a mutual fund. The cost of the fee can vary by the type of transaction, how many transactions you make, how much you have in assets under management, and even how you make it (i.e., online or via phone). Plenty of commission-free ETFs exist.

ACCOUNT SERVICE FEE: This is similar to the monthly service fee a bank charges on a checking or savings account. It's often an annual fee and may get waived if you hit a certain threshold for assets under management or if you waive paper statements and elect for electronic-only communication.

FRONT-END LOAD OR BACK-END LOAD: You pay a fee for the purchase (front-end load) or sale (back-end load) of your mutual fund investment. The fees for load funds usually pay the broker or advisor who researched the fund, advised you to purchase it, and placed the buy order for you. Back-end loads may be reduced or phased out depending on how long you hold the fund. DIY investors typically avoid investing in a load fund.

REDEMPTION FEE: This is separate from the back-end load fee, but also gets charged when you sell your shares in a fund. This fee is charged to offset the cost the brokerage may incur when selling your shares.

PURCHASE FEE: A fee you're charged when you buy shares in a fund. This is separate from the front-end load fee because, like a redemption fee, it is used to cover the cost of the transaction.

NO-LOAD FUNDS: There is no fee to buy into or sell your investment in a mutual fund. The expense ratios on no-load funds are typically lower than that of their load-fund counterparts. The fewer and lower the fees, the more you pocket.

12B-1 FEE: Another fee your brokerage may charge to offset the operational costs of running a mutual fund. It is baked into the expense ratio, so you may not notice it at first, but it will push the overall cost of the expense ratio up. The 12b-1 fee is capped at 1 percent by FINRA (the Financial Industry Regulatory Authority). One percent may not sound like much, but that can really eat away at your returns, so check to see if a fund comes with a 12b-1 fee before making the purchase.

IS MY MONEY PROTECTED?

Well, that's a bit of a tricky question, with an answer of both yes and no.

"Definitely safe, as long as the firm is SEC and FINRA registered and has SIPC* [Securities Investor Protection Corporation] insurance, which all the firms basically are required to have," says Alex Benke. "The common worry is that the firm is newer and will fold, and then what happens to my money? It's different than a bank folding because you'll get the shares back and will then just have to put them in a less fancy account."

This process of moving your shares is known as an "in-kind transfer." Let's say you've bought three shares of Netflix through Trusty Investing (a fictional robo-advisor). Trusty Investing folds after a year and you switch over to using a different brokerage firm: Reliable. You haven't lost your claim to those three shares of Netflix because you, not Trusty, are the owner of those shares. You'll just need to transfer the shares to your new brokerage account at Reliable.

SIPC insurance is similar to the FDIC insurance you get from a bank. As of 2018, it protects consumers with coverage of up to $500,000 for all accounts you have at the same institution, with a maximum of $250,000 for cash. This protection is for if the financial institution you use to invest fails. This is not to be confused with what happens if your investments lose value. Which takes us to the no part of this answer.

The stock market goes up and down. There will be days when your investments lose money, so no, your money isn't entirely protected. You may one day take a risk that doesn't pay off in the short term or maybe at

---

*If your brokerage is an SIPC member and ends up in financial trouble, the SIPC insurance will help protect you against losses. However, it doesn't bail you out if the market takes a tumble. You can learn more at https://www.sipc.org/for-investors/what-sipc-protects.

all. That's why diversifying, rebalancing, and considering your time horizon are critical. You need to mitigate the fallout you'll experience from the inevitable downturns, market corrections, and recessions.

CHECKLIST FOR GETTING STARTED

❑ Set your goal:

  • Why are you investing?

❑ Determine your risk tolerance:

  • How much risk are you willing to take with this money?

❑ Decide on your time horizon:

  • When do you want to use the money?

❑ Collect all your personal information:

  • Social Security or tax identification number, government-issued ID, bank account information, personal and financial information

❑ Decide what kind of account you'd like to open:

  • Retirement, saving for education costs, general savings

❑ Compare fees:

  • Are you getting value for the cost of the expense ratio and any other fees you're paying? Or are you looking for the lowest-cost version of a fund?

❑ Pick a brokerage firm.

❑ Pick a type of investment.

Chapter 7

I Like Gambling—
Isn't That Like Individual Stock Picking?

"BUY WHAT YOU KNOW." It's super-cliché investing advice, but it's an adage I took to heart when making my first stock pick.

As a long-term index fund investor myself, this book is part of the reason I decided I should at least try out individual stock picking. (We're not talking day-trader-level stuff.) Instead of going for some of the low-hanging fruit of things I knew, like buying some shares of Netflix or Amazon, I went with an oddball choice.

My dad works in the lithium industry. As a seven-year-old, I could parrot fun facts about lithium being the lightest metal on the periodic table of elements and that it's used in batteries and depression medication. I probably freaked out some grown-ups with that one, but come on, Nirvana had an entire song about lithium!

Anyway, lithium has been on something of a hot streak in the last decade, as evidenced by the rise of companies like Tesla and the interest in green energy. I even had an interesting experience doing PR for a company that built battery-storage facilities for storing renewable energy.

Suffice it to say, for not working in the lithium industry, I had some familiarity with the product.

So, when deciding which stock to buy, I went with a lithium-related option. And let me tell you, it's been quite the volatile ride.

I invested about $5,000 in the stock. Five grand is certainly not chump change, but it was also an amount of money I could stomach losing if everything went sideways. In three months, it had doubled in value. By six months, my $5,000 investment had risen to over $14,000. Man, was my first stock-picking rodeo going better than I could've imagined. Then it stopped its upward trajectory and began to backslide. The investment dropped from $14,000 to $7,000 in four months, but I was still up by over $2,000. Even though that's still a nice chunk of change, it was painful to look at the graph and see how much it had fallen since its peak.

However, this stock choice was a buy-and-hold strategy for me, just like much of my index fund investing. So, what will ultimately happen remains to be seen.

PICKING INDIVIDUAL STOCKS . . . IF YOU MUST

It's been mentioned a few times already in this book that individual stock picking should not be your primary means of investing. In fact, for many, it shouldn't even be a contender. However, I'm not about to write an investing book for beginners without addressing it. So, here it is. I will give you information about *how* to pick individual stocks, but that by no means should indicate that I think it's a wise financial move for the average rookie investor. Most seasoned investors don't get down with day trading, and many don't even dabble in individual stocks.

"I did day trading before, and it drove me insane," says Ashley Fox, a financial education specialist. "I'm too busy to day-trade, so I'm a long-term investor. My favorite holding period is forever."

But you may be convinced that, at some point, you'll want to purchase some individual stocks. (I mean, I did, so who am I to chastise the choice?) Here's what you should know.

The Most Important Consideration: Could You Withstand Losing It All?

We've been discussing diversification, risk tolerance, asset allocation, and goal setting ad nauseam throughout this book by this point. And you'll just keep hearing about them, too, because they are critical parts of building an investing portfolio that will weather the ups and downs of the stock market. They are how you sustainably build wealth. Individual stock picking is deliberately not mentioned as one of the best ways for the average investor to build wealth because when you consider individual stock picking, you need to be prepared for one thing: could you withstand losing it all?

"[Stock picking] is an entire job," says Colleen Jaconetti, CFP®, senior investment analyst for Vanguard Investment Strategy Group. "You have to know: Is it a strong company? What's going on in the industry? What's going on that could impact the product that people are putting out? How is the company managed? Unless you really have the time to do the analysis on the company and the industry, to know all the factors that impact that company, it's very difficult to pick one company or another."

Even though Jaconetti doesn't recommend focusing on individual stock picking as a significant part of your portfolio, she certainly understands the appeal: "When my husband and I got married, he was in IT and wanted to invest in Cisco. So, we took a small amount of money and invested in Cisco because that was important to him. But, for the most part, that's not part of our long-term investment portfolio. That is truly his 'I'm passionate about this company, I love it, I've been reading about it for three years, and I really want to do this.' Okay. But I certainly wouldn't let him do that with our financial future."

Even those who make stock picking their full-time jobs don't always outperform the market index. In fact, they often don't. A cat has been shown to be a better stock picker. Okay, so it didn't use the scientific method—but a goofy contest run by the *Observer* back in 2012 pitted a cat named Orlando against a panel of professional traders[1] (specifically, a wealth manager, a stock broker, and a fund manager) and students from a secondary school. Three teams (two human; the third, the feline) started out with £5,000 each to invest in five stocks from the FTSE All-Share Index. The humans picked stocks based on experience, knowledge, and, supposedly, skill, while the cat threw a toy mouse at a grid of numbers that corresponded to potential stock choices. Each quarter, all the teams could exchange any stocks from the index. By the end of the fourth quarter, Orlando increased his portfolio 4.2 percent, to £5,542.60, compared to the team of trained professionals' £5,176.60.

HOLD UP, IS INDIVIDUAL STOCK PICKING LIKE GAMBLING?

"People need to have the right attitude for investing," says Dave Nugent, head of investments for Wealthsimple, "and not treat the stock market like the lottery or Vegas. They need to realize when they're investing in the stock market, they're actually investing in real companies that sell real products and provide real service to people. I think it's easy to get caught up in the fast pace of the market."

The stock market so often gets compared to gambling because neither one promises guaranteed returns. It's not an apt comparison, though, even for individual stock picking, and it's one that's likely to make investors bristle a bit.

For one thing, being an investor means you own a piece of the company—no matter how small. Putting a $100 bet down at the blackjack table at the Venetian doesn't mean you've purchased $100 worth of ownership in the Venetian.

Both require levels of risk analysis, but what happens when you win big in Vegas? You should cash out. Quit while you're ahead. The house is supposed to always win, and the game is rigged against you. If you keep playing, then you're going to lose your money.

Investing is pretty much the opposite. You're supposed to take the long view and ride the ups and downs. On average, the market yields healthy returns for those who stay in. Granted, that advice is typically for a well-diversified portfolio and not exclusively for individual stock pick-ing, but it can be true for individual stocks if you're taking well-researched positions and have a buy-and-hold strategy as opposed to day trading.

Perhaps a big windfall from investing produces a similar euphoric high as one you'd get on the floor of a casino, but investing and gambling are not synonymous.

HOW IS STOCK PICKING DIFFERENT FROM OTHER TYPES OF INVESTING?

"If you think about investing in individual securities, it's risky because you are investing in the success of one company or a handful of companies," explains Maria Bruno, CFP®, a senior investment analyst for Vanguard In-vestment Strategy Group. "And what's happening then, potentially, is that you are pivoting away from the general broad market. So, when you see the market movements, your individual portfolio might perform quite differently because you're invested in one or two or a handful of securi-ties. So just be really careful in terms of how much you own in individual securities."

PUTTING YOUR TOE IN THE WATER WITH FRACTIONAL SHARES

Plenty of experts will caution you against buying individual stocks, but Avi Lele, founder and CEO of Stockpile, sees individual stocks as a way to get people in the investing game. Stockpile, an online investing ser-vice, is a way for investors to buy, sell, and even gift fractional shares of stocks.

For example, Sam wants to buy stock in Bamzon, except Bamzon is currently trading at $1,400 for a single share. He doesn't have that kind of money, but he could purchase $100 worth of Bamzon, which would mean he'd own around 7 percent of a share. If Bamzon started to pay dividends to its investors, then Sam would receive 7 percent of a dividend.

Buying fractional shares isn't particularly common because the stock market doesn't trade in fractions. What Stockpile does as a brokerage is it buys the entire share and then holds the leftover fraction. When Sam placed his order for 7 percent of Bamzon, Stockpile purchased the entire share at $1,400. On the same day, Mary placed an order for 40 percent of Bamzon, Jake bought 30 percent, and Tony purchased 5 percent. After all those purchases, Stockpile held the remaining 18 percent of the share.

The value of individual stocks has a few angles, explains Avi Lele. "The first thing we find is that it's the thing that gets you to get started. It's hard to get excited about a nameless, faceless ETF or mutual fund. Whereas everyone has brand affinity, so the thing we find is that people come in through brand affinity. They basically say, 'I didn't know I could own Facebook stock. I know a lot about that company, or I'm a big user of Nike products, so let me buy some Nike stock.' That's the thing that makes the on-ramp really easy for people. They've got at least one thing they understand, which is the actual company that they're investing in.

"But that doesn't mean that now they should embark on a path of only buying individual stocks. It often makes a lot of sense to branch out into ETFs. If you can take an ETF and kind of bring out what specifically the ETF does, like supporting the troops or clean-and-green, then you can teach people along the way this is what's in the ETF. This particular ETF has stocks that translate into defense contractors and other military-type companies, while this other ETF is solar and wind and companies like that. The same thing that tends to work for stocks also works really well for ETFs.

"Some people start off saying, 'I just want to buy an S&P 500 ETF and just get that bedrock foundational investment in place, and then I can add to it with other things that I feel like would be good investments.' Whereas other people on the other end of the spectrum start off with an individual stock and keep diversifying their individual stock portfolio.

It's another equally valid way to diversify. Either way, all the rules apply. Start early, diversify, do it regularly, and do it for the long haul."

DECIDING WHICH STOCK TO PICK

So, you've decided it's time to add some individual stocks to your portfolio. It could be because you see real value in a particular company or that you're curious about the experience. Either way, here are some questions you should be able to answer when deciding which stock to pick.

How Much in Total Do You Want to Spend?

"Don't put all your eggs in one basket," says Vanguard's Maria Bruno, CFP®. "It's very natural for individuals to have the desire to hold some individual securities. While that may be fine, don't let it be a large part of the portfolio. I sometimes say, 'Have a little bucket of play money.' And don't let that impact your overall portfolio."

Can You Afford to Buy Even One Share?

Before you make a decision about which company stock you want to buy based on knowing, using, and understanding the product—you should probably check its share price. There are plenty of companies with shares that cost hundreds or upward of a thousand dollars.

Are You Still Diversified in Your Picks?

You still need to be diversifying. Even if you decide to go all-in on buying individual stocks and not to include a mutual fund or ETF in your portfolio (100 percent advising that this *not* be your strategy), then you shouldn't go all-in on one particular stock or even one sector.

Avi Lele understands the pressure of having all your money in one stock: "I finally had enough money and enough courage to go in and hope I didn't screw it up. I bought fifty shares of Microsoft, and then I was just a little overextended. I was in one stock, and it was at least a company I understood. I remember the share price, it was like $98, so I was in with just under $5,000. I was sitting there sweating it out every day, thinking, 'I hope it doesn't go down.'"

Had he been more diversified, it could've helped reduce his panic.

Have You Researched the Company?

This shouldn't be a "trust your gut" decision. You need to back up your feelings with at least a rudimentary analysis of the company.

- Is it profitable?
    - A company's corporate report can give you details on its finances. Companies often have to file this information with the SEC, so you may be able to find it on the company's website or at SEC.gov.

- Is it reputable?
    - You may not know what's happening inside the company, but whistle-blowing has become increasingly common in recent years. Just searching the news usually lets you know about prior or current scandals.

- What's the history of returns?
    - Go to Morningstar and look up the stock you want to buy and check its chart to see the company's growth.

Do You Understand What the Company Does?

It's not imperative that you understand all the inner workings of the company, but you should at least be able to explain what it does. This strategy can prevent you from chasing the latest hot tip and ensure you're investing in something you understand. Bitcoin is a great example of people dumping money into a commodity they may not have understood just because everyone else was doing it. Those who understood block-chain could make well-researched, calculated investments. Those that didn't were simply throwing money into an investment.

Don't Invest Based on What Everyone Else Is Doing

It's easy to get caught up in the frenzy of a hot commodity. Try to avoid buying in when your friends, family, dentist, and the random person you started chatting with on the street all recommend one particular stock, because that means the price is going up! You don't want to buy when the share price is high.

WHAT YOU NEED TO KNOW IN ORDER TO BUY A STOCK

The first time I opened up a brokerage account with the intention of buying a specific stock, I had to spend about thirty minutes looking up definitions before I could take a half-assed, semi-educated guess at how to place the order. I remember looking at all the options and thinking, "I don't know! I just want to buy $5,000 worth of this stock! HOW HARD IS THAT TO DO?!"

Here are the things you may need to know before you log in to buy stock through your brokerage:

- The name/symbol of the stock
  - Okay, this one is fairly obvious and simple to find.

- The action you want to take
  - You'll probably have the option to buy, sell, or short-sell. In this case, you want to buy.

- How many shares you want to purchase
  - The platform you pick will likely offer a calculator to help you figure out how many shares. You plug in the amount

you want to spend, and it'll tell you how many shares that equals at the current market price. If there's no calculator, then it's pretty easy for you to figure out yourself. Let's say the stock you want to purchase costs $5 per share and you have $100 to invest. You'll want to buy twenty shares.

- The order type
  - *Market order:* You want to buy the stock, period. You're willing to do this at the best price available, which is whatever the market is currently dictating. By placing a market order you guarantee that you'll make the purchase, but you won't be guaranteeing the price.
  - *Limit order:* A limit order does the reverse of a market order. You guarantee a price maximum that you're willing to pay, but there's not a guarantee the order will successfully get placed. Limit orders can be used as a buyer and as a seller. Limit orders can also mitigate the risk of paying a higher price than expected, which can happen with a market order.
  - *Stop-loss order:* There is a buy stop-loss order and a sell stop-loss order. With a buy stop-loss order you place an order above the prevailing market price on the stock. If the stock hits your price, then the order you placed will become a market order and get placed at the next available price. With a stop-loss order, you can decide how much you're comfortable with a stock drop before you're willing to sell. This can remove some of your emotional attachment to an investment. Let's say you bought ten shares of Mosbius Designs at $30 per share, but if the stock falls more than 15 percent, you want to sell it off because you aren't willing to risk more than a 15 percent loss on it. You then set a stop-loss order for $25.50. If Mosbius Designs hits $25.50, then your broker will sell the ten shares for you. Once your stop-loss order is reached, then

it converts into a market order and will be sold at the next available price. This could cause a problem as you could end up buying or selling at a different price than you wanted.

- *Stop-limit order:* The stop-limit order combines the limit order with the stop-loss order. This means you set your stop price, or the price at which you want to buy or sell the stock, but you also set a limit price. You were willing to buy Mosbius Designs at $30, but if it hits $35, you no longer want to place the order. Similar to the limit order, you are not guaranteed that this transaction will execute.

- Timing

  - *Day only:* Your request to purchase will expire at the end of the trading day if it's not filled. (This is usually the default.)

  - *Good until cancelled:* Your request will live on for usually thirty to ninety days, or until it's been fulfilled or cancelled.

  - *Fill or kill:* The request to purchase is either immediately fulfilled in its entirety or cancelled. For example, you want to buy 200 shares of Mosbius Designs at $15 per share. Your broker isn't able to fulfill this order for you, so it gets cancelled.

  - *Immediate or cancel:* You want the trade immediately filled, either entirely or partially. Whatever isn't filled is cancelled. You still want 200 shares of Mosbius Designs at $15 per share, but your broker is only able to get 120 shares for $15 per share. She buys those for you and cancels the remainder of the order.

- What you want to do with your dividends

  - The platform I use requires you to opt in by checking a box next to "reinvest dividends," which would be easy to overlook. Some investments may not allow you to reinvest your dividends.

- Whether there are commissions and/or trading fees
  - Be sure to calculate that into the total cost of your purchase.

- How your transaction is being funded
  - You might have a cash reserve set up with your brokerage—fine. But if money is getting pulled out of your bank account to fund the purchase, then it could take a few business days to complete the order. That can make a world of difference when it comes to share prices.

GETTING SOME EXPERIENCE BEFORE YOU TRULY COMMIT

Tela Holcomb, an independent trader and the founder of the investing program Trade Your 9 to 5, started her stock-picking journey in the virtual world.

"I started in a practice account," says Holcomb. "That's a huge tool for beginners who don't know what they're doing in the beginning and are scared and don't want to lose money trying to learn."

Practice accounts may not be quite as prevalent as they used to be, but you can still find some online where you even compete against other people with virtual cash. Investopedia offers its Stock Market Game and TD Ameritrade offers paperMoney® for dabbling in virtual cash. Just make sure you read all the terms and conditions before you sign up, to ensure you're not going to start getting charged.

SHOULD I PURCHASE MY EMPLOYER'S STOCK?

Outside of an employer-sponsored retirement plan, you may also have the benefit of purchasing company stock. Oftentimes you're able to get access to this stock at a lower-than-market-value price, which makes it a deal. Still, company stock should be only a small part of your overall portfolio.

"Avoid concentrated investments," says Jaconetti, noting overinvesting in company stock as an example. "When you buy company stock, your financial future with your salary is highly tied to that company already. You double down almost by then buying a lot of company stock. It's just putting that much more of your future in that company's hands."

WHERE CAN I BUY STOCKS?

It's not terribly complicated to find where to buy stocks. You can go through most major brokerage firms and just place the order online. You don't have to call up an individual stock broker you hire in order to place the buy. You should compare commissions and fees, though, if you're trying to decide which brokerage firm to use. Options to consider include: Ally Invest, Charles Schwab, E*Trade, Fidelity, Merrill Edge, and TD Ameritrade.

While robo-advisors do use ETFs to build portfolios, not many of them provide an option for purchasing individual stocks. Robinhood is one app that does.

CHECKLIST FOR BUYING INDIVIDUAL STOCKS

❏ Are you okay losing all the money you're about to invest in an individual stock?

- Picking an individual stock to buy doesn't protect your downside in the same way investing in an index fund or ETF would, so you need to be emotionally and financially prepared to lose money.

❏ Do your research and thoroughly vet the company before making the purchase.

❏ Pick a brokerage firm.

  • Don't forget to compare commissions and trading fees.

❏ Decide how much you're going to invest and how you're going to place the order.

  • Do you want to do a market order, limit order, stop-loss order, or stop-limit order?

❏ Determine ahead of time if this is a buy-and-hold purchase and then remind yourself of your goal in order to emotionally handle volatility.

Chapter 8

Investing—
Of Course There's an App for That

IN 2013, when I opened my first taxable account, you generally needed to have at least a few thousand dollars saved in order to open up an index fund or ETF with a traditional brokerage. That's only five years prior to my writing the words on this page, and yet micro-investing apps weren't available at the time. It's amazing how quickly technology is changing the way we're able to enter the markets. By 2014, the landscape of investing had already started changing. Suddenly, there were options for people to invest with only a few bucks via an app on their smartphones.

Today, there are a variety of ways to invest with minimal sums of money. Some are gamified, while others adhere to the old principles of investing, but they all democratize the process to make it accessible to anyone with a bank account and a couple spare dollars a month.

WHAT IS MICRO-INVESTING?

It feels like such a Millennial cliché—of course "there's an app for that" when it comes to investing! Micro-investing apps solved a common problem for young, rookie investors: investment minimums. Not only can it be cost-prohibitive to purchase a single share of some stocks, but some mutual funds can also require a minimum investment of $1,000 to $3,000 to even as high as $10,000 in some cases.

As the name implies, micro-investing only requires you to deposit little bits of money at a time into your investment. This is often done in an automated or similarly simple manner for you, the user, in order to both reduce stress and actually encourage you to keep investing.

Just like robo-advisors, micro-investing apps offer a variety of tools and ways in which you can be investing. You could be doing individual stock picking or build a portfolio out of ETFs. You generally create a portfolio by answering a few questions about your goals and risk tolerance, and then the app will recommend investments.

Micro-investing apps are not the same as your brokerage firm's app. These are companies built around the idea of helping people get into investing with as little as a few dollars, but ultimately you can level up, too.

WHAT YOU NEED TO KNOW AND SHARE BEFORE YOU START

Just like signing up with a brokerage, you'll need to fill out some information in order to invest via an app. Here are some of the things you need to be prepared to provide:

- Email address
- Full, legal name
- Date of birth
  - You must be eighteen or older to have an account in your name. Otherwise, a parent or guardian may be able to open a custodial account for you.
- Social Security number
- Phone number and address
- Your citizenship status:
  - Some apps are only available to US citizens.

- Other information:
  - When filling out the investor profile, you'll be asked some basic questions like: employment status, annual income, perceived risk tolerance level (conservative, moderate, aggressive), and net worth.
- How will you fund the account?
  - You'll need to link a bank account and/or credit or debit card to your app. This is how you'll add money to your investments. You'll also need to verify that you're the owner of the checking account. Typically, this is done by the app making two small deposits in your account. (They later take the money back.) You log in to the app and enter what those deposit amounts were.

A LOOK AT MICRO-INVESTING APPS

It's important to actually overview some micro-investing apps in order to best help you understand what they have to offer. However, these apps and their services tend to evolve rather quickly. The information that follows is from the summer of 2018.

Before using any of this information to actually select and use a micro-investing app, it's important to research the company yourself and check current functionality and fees. This overview is just to give you a sense of how these apps work.

As always, make sure anything you use to invest is SIPC protected.

Acorns

Acorns is a perfect match for the true beginner looking to get help building a well-diversified portfolio. Seasoned investors can get plenty of value from Acorns, but its simplicity makes it great for the true rookie.

What It Offers

- *Investment options:* You can invest in one of five available portfolios.
- *Invest your spare change:* Acorn's tagline is "Invest your spare change. Anyone can grow wealth." The invest-your-spare-change philosophy manifests in the "Round-Ups." You can set the app to round up your purchases to the next dollar and invest the difference. If you bought a coffee for $1.65, then it can round up your purchase to $2 and invest the $0.35.
- *Automatic investments:* You can also elect to set up automatic deposits into your investments. This can be done daily, weekly, or monthly.
- *Found Money™:* This works like a cash-back portal. By clicking through Acorns to shop with brand partners, a percentage of your purchase will be credited to your Acorn account. For example, let's say Barnes & Noble is a brand partner and offers 2 percent back. You need to buy a book. You open your Acorns app and go to the "Found Money" screen. You locate Barnes & Noble and then click on it to be redirected to the Barnes & Noble website. After you place your order, 2 percent of its value will be credited to your Acorns account within a set period of time after purchase.
- *Education component:* "Education goes hand in hand with investing," says Jennifer Barrett, chief education officer for Acorns, which offers a stand-alone financial education site and integrates education into the tool. "Because we recognize so many people [who] are investing with Acorns have probably never done it before, certainly not outside of a 401(k), we make it very easy to start investing, and we help people along the learning curve. Then you see them start to become more engaged users and put more money in."
- *Other:* The app also offers Acorns Later and Acorns Spend, to help with retirement and day-to-day spending. Acorns Later gives you the option to invest in a Roth, Traditional, or SEP IRA. Acorns helps build your plan based on your lifestyle and goals. Acorns

Spend is a checking account and debit card integrated with Acorns that allows roundups to happen in real time.

Available Investments

- Acorns keeps this pretty streamlined. You choose from among five portfolios, all of which are invested in ETFs from well-known investment management companies like Vanguard and BlackRock. The portfolio options are: conservative, moderately conservative, moderate, moderately aggressive, and aggressive.

Costs

- $1 per month for Acorns accounts under $1 million, or free for college students.
- $2 per month for Acorns + Acorns Later (the retirement portfolio).
- $3 per month for Acorns + Acorns Later + Acorns Spend.

Robinhood

The tongue-in-cheek name for a folk hero who robbed from the rich and gave to the poor perfectly aligns with Robinhood's slogan: "Investing. Now for the rest of us." Robinhood can certainly be used by absolute rookies, but it's better suited for those looking to do individual stock picking and even dabble in cryptocurrency and options trading.

What It Offers

- *Stocks and ETFs*: More than 5,000 stocks and the majority of ETFs listed on the major US exchanges.
- *Robinhood Crypto*: In 2018, Robinhood made cryptocurrency available for buying and selling in eighteen US states. It wasn't available nationwide due to state regulations. At the time of this writing, it supported buying and selling Bitcoin, Bitcoin Cash, Dogecoin, Ethereum, and Litecoin.
- *Options trading:* This one is a bit more technical to explain, but in short, you're making a bet on the future price of a commodity and

will then have the ability to purchase it at a particular price and sell it for an immediate profit. For example, Fab Five Inc. is currently trading at $23 per share. You're pretty certain it will increase in value, so you buy a "call option" for 100 shares. The call option costs you $1 per share, so $100, and allows you to buy 100 shares of Fab Five Inc. at $25 per share (also known as the "strike price") within the next sixty days. Fab Five Inc. does increase in value to $28 per share within the sixty days. You then buy the 100 shares at $25 and immediately sell them for a $3 profit per share (less the $100 you spent on purchasing the call option).

- *Robinhood Gold:* A trading option that allows an investor to buy "on margin," which, in this case, means buying with money loaned to you by Robinhood Financial. You also get extended trading hours and can trade thirty minutes before the market opens and two hours after it closes.

Costs

- Trading is commission free, but there are fees charged by the SEC and FINRA. Robinhood doesn't pocket any of those fees, but you should expect to see them as part of your trade.

At this point, you should be wondering how Robinhood makes money. According to its website,[1] it does charge $6 per month for members who opt into Robinhood Gold. The company also earns revenue by collecting interest on the cash and securities held in Robinhood accounts.

Stash

Stash is a good fit for a beginner who wants to be a little more hands-on about picking investments or has specific preferences on the type of companies he or she invests in. Of Stash's customers, 86 percent are first-time or beginner investors, according to Brandon Krieg, CEO and cofounder.

What It Offers

"We started with education and rolled out investing in a taxable account, and then we rolled out retire, and then we rolled out custodial, and now we['ve] announced we're building banking services," says Krieg. "We're really just trying to holistically give advice and education to better the lives of our customers."

- *Investments:* You can build your own portfolio by selecting ETFs and/or stocks aligned with your goals. Stash does offer a coach to help with your selection if you need. There is also a gamification aspect in which you earn points, which are kind of like gold stars, for achieving certain steps, like making a deposit, setting up Auto-Stash (automatic deposits into your investments), and then for selecting certain stocks, bonds, and ETFs that align with creating a diversified portfolio.
- *Stash Retire:* You can invest in a traditional or Roth IRA for a minimum of $5. The requirements are the same as investing in an IRA through a brokerage, as specified by IRS income restrictions and contribution limits.
- *StashLearn:* Stash's education component is free to all on the app's website. You can find articles on topics varying from basic personal finance to more technical investing advice.
- *Banking:* Stash also moved into the banking business with Stash Checking, a checking account powered by Green Dot.
- *Custodial:* Custodial accounts allow parents to open investing accounts for children under the age of eighteen.

Available Investments

- Stash offers access to more than one hundred investments, including ETFs and individual stocks. ETFs have been categorized with "Stash-ified" names to make it easier for you to understand what you'd be investing in. For example, "Social Media Mania" provides holdings in social media companies. Stash also offers information about the fund manager and the risk tolerance. For example, the "Blue Chip" fund is made up of some of the biggest companies in the United States (e.g., Apple, Facebook, Microsoft); it's a conservative fund that's managed by Vanguard. You can also invest in fractional shares of individual stocks. (Fractional shares are explained in chapter 7.)

Costs
- $1 per month with no commission on accounts under $5,000 for Stash Invest and $2 per month for Stash Retire.
- 0.25 percent per year of the portfolio for accounts of $5,000 or more. (Example: a $10,000 account would be charged $25 annually.)

Stockpile
Similar to Robinhood, Stockpile is for investors who want to add individual stocks to their portfolio or to gift stocks to others.

What It Offers
- *Investments:* You can purchase or gift (with gift cards) fractional stocks and you can also purchase ETFs. You can also set up a recurring deposit into your investments to buy more shares and reinvest dividends when applicable.
- *Custodial accounts:* Parents can gift their kids fractional shares in their favorite companies.

Available Investments
- There are more than 1,000 stocks and ETFs in which you can invest, but the entire market is not at your disposal. If there's a small, niche company in which you want to invest, then you may need to go through a larger brokerage.

Cost

- It costs $0.99 to buy a stock and the same price to sell if you purchased it with cash from your account. There is a 3 percent fee if you use a credit or debit card.
- No monthly fees or minimums.
- Purchasing a gift card is more expensive because you're covering the trading commission and fees for the recipient: $2.99 for the first stock + $0.99 for each additional stock + 3 percent for credit or debit card fees (so the recipient doesn't have to pay anything when redeeming the gift card).

AN IMPORTANT POINT ABOUT COST

It's really easy to look at a fee like $1 per month and think, "Pshh, that's nothing!" In the scheme of what $1 can normally buy you, yeah, it sounds like a great value. However, you still need to consider how fees can eat away at your returns. If you're only investing a tiny bit of money each month, then $1 can represent a significant portion of your portfolio and diminish or completely negate your actual returns.

For example, if you only invest $5 per month, that's $60 per year before any compound interest. Even if an 8 percent return is compounded monthly, you would at best add about $2 to your investments. The $12 (i.e., $1 per month) you paid in fees just ate away all your returns. Now, if you put something like $25 into your account per month, you're going to come out ahead. It doesn't take a huge chunk of change to reap the rewards, but it needs to be more than just a few bucks a month. Krieg noted that the average person using Auto-Stash puts away $25 a week. That's $100 a month!

There may not be additional trading fees or commissions, but you'll still have to pay an expense ratio* on any fund in your portfolio. Your

---

*You can go back to chapter 6 for a refresher course on expense ratios and fees.

app doesn't usually cover that cost for you. It's often already reflected in the price you see when you make the purchase, but it's important for you to know that you are still paying an expense ratio. Using an app to invest isn't a way to bypass an expense ratio on an ETF.

COMMON MISCONCEPTIONS ABOUT MICRO-INVESTING

As with any relatively new technology, there are always going to be misconceptions about capabilities. Acorns, for instance, was launched in August 2014, and Stash was founded about six months later, in February 2015. Barrett of Acorns and Stash's Krieg hope to correct some of the misinformation.

Addressing the claim that Acorns is "a starter app," Barrett concedes that "it's a very simple interface, but the machinery behind it is quite complex. So, we have five portfolios to keep it simple, but we invest across seven exchange-traded funds that have more than seven thousand stocks and bonds. And we're always recalibrating based on market movements. It's based on modern portfolio theory; it's actually pretty complex. I've been investing for a while now, and [I] invest in a lot of different things, and I have a good chunk of change in Acorns because it's just a smart portfolio, and it's fractional investing. You're spreading the risk. We're not the only app that does fractional investing, and we're not the only one that rebalances your portfolio or reinvests your dividends, but I think the combination of those three things and the roundups and making it so effortless to continue to put a little more in each month is an unusual combination."

"I hear people say, 'Well, if you don't have a lot of money, you shouldn't be investing,'" says Stash's Krieg. "That's fine for wealthy people to think, but it's not true. If you consistently make a habit of saving and investing and you do it on a regular basis, over the long run, it works. There are so many people missing out on an opportunity by not doing it. Small amounts of money do add up, and some people just don't see it. They think you have to be rich to start. The other thing I think about a lot is the data on how the Millennial generation is missing out on such a huge opportunity because they're afraid of the stock market and afraid of investing. There's a lot of data on how many millions of dollars they'll be missing out on in retirement by not saving. You can start when you're really young."

JUST BECAUSE YOU CAN, DOES THAT MEAN YOU SHOULD?

We rely on apps for a lot these days. Much of our lives has been streamlined with the use of technology. Everything from transportation to ordering food to documenting our thoughts is all done via our smartphones. But should such a critical piece of your financial life be something you're doing with the touch of a button?

"I think it's dope," says Ashley Fox, financial education specialist and founder of Empify. "People are coming up with a million unique ways to get people to invest, but they're using the emotional way. Let's consider the 401(k). People don't think about the 401(k) because they never [see] the money. They're still investing, but because they didn't see the money first, they don't feel like someone is taking it from them. [Apps] are dope because it unconsciously allows people to build wealth gradually.

"I talked to someone the other day, and he said, 'I only have a couple dollars, I can't invest because it won't make a difference.' I said, 'Okay, if I [gave] you a dollar a week, for the next twenty years, would you take it?' and they say, 'Yeah!' I ask why. He said, 'Because it's money, and over time, I'll have a lot of money.' I said, 'Okay, but you just told me a dollar was pointless, so now you're telling me a dollar actually matters to you.'

"We have to remove the 'Oh, this is only a little bit or it's not enough.' Because it's not as simple as 'Hey, you need to invest, go do it.' Sometimes we need to do these emotional things that trick us into unconsciously building wealth, and I think that's a great way to do it."

Jill Schlesinger would prefer you to consider investing as just a part of life, like health—and we gamify health with tools like step trackers. "Anything that gets you going, do it! Anything," she says.

Schlesinger does point out that you need to do more than just opting in to options like rounding up, but acknowledges it can be a helpful first step.

LITTLE BITS HELP, BUT YOU NEED TO DO MORE

I engage in a really quirky savings strategy: I save $5 bills. Each time I pay for an item in cash and get a $5 bill with my change, I go home and put that bill in a jar. It's a silly savings strategy I read about once and decided to try. Within a year, I'd saved about $1,000 I probably wouldn't have had otherwise. Now, this isn't my main means of saving, of course. It's just an additional challenge I use to level up my savings goal. All the $5 bills I saved went right into my honeymoon fund.

Just putting a few dollars into a micro-investing app is the same thing as my $5-bill-saving gimmick. It's a nice addition, but not enough to be your core strategy.

Getting started is important, but eventually you also must put in the effort to level up, which isn't hard to do with these apps. You could be building genuine wealth using a micro-investing app because most of these apps make it possible for you to do so right in the app with automatic contributions, but you have to take the initiative. Investing your spare change alone or putting aside five to ten dollars a month alone is not going to accomplish your wealth goals.

Now, if an app is something you're using for that little bit of extra edge, in addition to contributing to your 401(k) and putting automatic contributions into a taxable account at a brokerage—then, by all means, you do you. But if you're using an investing app as your main means of building your portfolio, then it's on you to contribute more than a few dollars a week, especially as your financial health gets stronger and stronger. Just like how you'd need to proactively contribute each week or month to a regular brokerage or robo-advisor account.

CHECKLIST FOR MICRO-INVESTING

❑ Research the different app options available and decide which one is the right fit for both your style and your current investing needs.

❑ Take advantage of all the education platforms and tools available to you within the app.

❑ Do the math on costs. If you're only investing minute amounts of money, then you'll see even a small fee of $1 can quickly eat away at your returns.

❑ Don't just rely on gimmicks and gamifications within the apps. Set up recurring deposits to make sure you're actually starting to build wealth.

❑ Password-protect your smartphone and the app! You have sensitive personal and financial information on your smartphone. Make it at least a little bit more difficult for others to gain access by password-protecting both your phone and the app (using fingerprint identification or whatever new technology allows you to level up protection).

Chapter 9

Robo-Advisor or Human Advisor— Which Is Better?

A BATTLE IS BREWING in the investing industry, and it all centers around the answer to a key question: which is better, a robo-advisor or a human advisor?

The answer: it depends.

"It depends" is the infuriating but correct way to look at most things on your financial journey. There are so many factors at play, and each person must be evaluated according to his or her individual needs. A robo-advisor could be a perfect fit for you, but I might need a long-term relationship with a human advisor.

To be honest, I was highly skeptical of robo-advisors when they first started to gain traction. I admittedly have a dash of Luddite in me, but something just felt so off about the idea of being able to automate every aspect of a person's investing life. I had no faith that an algorithm could be taught the nuance necessary to build a person's portfolio for medium- and long-term financial goals. I feared it would just spit out the same answer for most people. But I was also giving many human advisors far too much credit, since some of them don't spend quality time with each individual client.

Besides, the anti-robo-investor mentality feels rooted in the archaic idea that investing is really complicated and that only super-smart Wall Street bros can understand what's going on. Blech.

I have no shame in admitting that I grossly misjudged robo-advisors, and they've significantly evolved in the last decade to better provide the nuance needed. In this chapter we'll figure out if a robo-advisor is a good fit for your investing journey.

Before we get started, here's the first thing you need to understand: a robo-advisor isn't just some algorithm making your investing decisions while you live your life. People are involved the entire way. And in some cases, you can even add in a human financial advisor when you have questions or after major life events unfold. It's not entirely dissimilar to using a discount brokerage firm where you can move from being a DIY investor to working with a professional. The underlying technology and the level of micromanaging on your end (think rebalancing and tax-loss harvesting) will be less with a robo-advisor than DIY-ing at a discount brokerage.

WHAT IS A ROBO-ADVISOR?

"The easiest way to get started," jokes Dave Nugent, head of investments for Wealthsimple. "A robo-advisor simplifies the way in which people save and invest for their futures and typically provides clean and easy experiences that help clients understand what they own and why they own it. It also allows anyone to automate a lot of the operational and administrative tasks that cost a lot of money in the traditional world."

"The term *robo-advisor* started meaning technology could manage your portfolio," says Alex Benke, CFP®, vice president of financial advice and planning for Betterment. "There are many people that misunderstand how the technology is being used. For example, we see the market will go down, and their account goes down, and they ask, 'How come your algorithms aren't dealing with this?' We don't have any algorithms that deal with that aside from tax-loss harvesting and things; there's no market-timing algorithm that's in there trying to make sure you don't lose money. I think terms like *robo-advisor* imply to uninformed people that there is some kind of bot doing things like that." He continues to explain that robo-advisors are actually "taking super-boring investing principles and enabling us to do that at scale with technology."

"*Robo-advisor* is a very generic term for all types of models," he adds. "There's [building a] portfolio, there's adding financial planning on top of that. There's the fact you can also get an actual advisor. We're one of a whole bunch of other firms that have all kinds of capabilities in terms of sophistication of financial planning. Some just have a calculator and some have very personalized financial planning advice. We all rebalance differently. We do tax-loss harvesting differently. Some have dedicated planners, and some have teams of planners."

IS *ROBO-ADVISOR* EVEN THE BEST TERM?

For simplicity's sake, I'll continue to use the word *robo-advisor* throughout this chapter. It's currently a widely used term, so I'm not going to fight against the vernacular you're used to hearing. However, Benke raised a fair point during our interview that the term *robo-advisor* gives investors a false impression of what many of the platforms do.

"I think the term is too narrow," says Benke. "People think of Betterment as a robo-advisor, and yet we have an offering that involves people [financial advisors] too. Of course, there are lots of people behind the [robo] offering as well. We think *online financial advisor* is a little more correct. Because it implies use of technology, but it doesn't pigeonhole in terms of how you're getting that advice. The same person who wants to do it themselves without an advisor initially should be able to change their mind at different phases in their life."

WHAT EXACTLY WOULD I BE SIGNING UP FOR?

Each robo-advisor is different in both offerings and pricing models. Many robo-advisors handle IRAs and 401(k)s, so even if you're only investing for retirement right now and not ready to put money into taxable accounts, you still could use a robo-advisor.

What follows is a high-level overview of the offerings of five robo-advisors. Generally, you will answer a few questions about where you are in life (e.g., your age and whether you're retired) and your goals, total assets, and risk tolerance levels, and then you'll be guided to various portfolio options based on your answers. Typically, you will then be invested in ETFs from various brokerages such as Vanguard, Fidelity, Schwab, and BlackRock.

These descriptions and price ranges are from the summer of 2018. You should always check company websites for the most up-to-date information, especially as competition in the marketplace is likely to impact offerings and pricing models.

Also, keep in mind that you're generally still charged the expense ratio for each individual fund. You may read "no trade or transaction fees," but most of the time that's after the expense ratio. The expense ratio isn't charged by your robo-advisor, it's charged by the fund specifically, so your robo-advisor isn't benefiting from or absorbing that fee for you. It is in your robo-advisor's best interest to put you in funds that charge the lowest-possible expense ratio, because an expense ratio eats away at overall returns.

Betterment

- Digital ($0 minimum balance with a 0.25 percent annual fee)
- Premium ($100,000 minimum balance with a 0.40 percent annual fee)

The Betterment Portfolio Strategy offers "a globally diversified mix of exchange-traded funds." Both the Digital and the Premium options offer low-cost, diversified investment portfolios with automatic rebalancing, and tax-loss harvesting strategies. The Digital platform offers access to licensed financial experts, while Premium gets you unlimited access to CFPs and in-depth advice on investments outside of Betterment, like a 401(k) or real estate.

Wealthsimple

- Basic ($0 minimum, 0.5 percent fees on $0–$99,999)
- Black ($100,000 minimum, 0.4 percent fee)

Wealthsimple also uses ETFs that track the global economy. Both levels offer auto deposits, rebalancing, tax-loss harvesting, dividend reinvesting, personalized portfolios, and human financial advice via call, text, or email. The Black level offers all the Basic-level features plus goal-based planning, dedicated financial planning, and increased tax efficiency.

Ellevest

- Digital ($0 minimum balance, 0.25 percent annual fee)
- Premium ($50,000 minimum balance, 0.50 percent annual fee)
- Private Wealth Management ($1,000,000 minimum balance with an annual fee based on assets under management)

Ellevest is run by women and geared toward women investors, but you don't have to be a woman in order to invest with Ellevest. It typically uses ETFs to help you build your portfolio. The Digital offering provides personalized investment portfolios with the option for automatic deposits, no-penalty withdrawals if you want to take your money out of Ellevest, automatic rebalancing, Ellevest's own tax-minimization methodology (tax-loss harvesting), and unlimited support from the Ellevest concierge team, which includes financial professionals. The Premium offering includes all the Digital perks plus one-on-one access to CFPs for personalized guidance and one-on-one access to executive coaches for help with career moves and negotiation.

Wealthfront

- 0.25 percent annual advisory fee for everyone

Wealthfront doesn't promote the use of financial advisors the same way some of its competitors do. It seems to lean in to the "robo-advisor" moniker a bit harder than its competitors by really focusing on the software and not adding a human touch. Even a philosophy on the homepage is "Technology can do some things better than people. We use software to better execute time-tested investment strategies." Like its competitors, Wealthfront focuses on goal setting, determining your risk tolerance, and then building a well-diversified portfolio around that information.

Swell

- 0.75 percent annual fee, $50 minimum account balance

Swell is a slightly different offering from your average robo-advisor because it focuses specifically on impact investing. At the time of this writing, you can choose from seven different portfolios: Green Tech, Zero Waste, Disease Eradication, Clean Water, Renewable Energy, Healthy Living, and Impact 400. It's a solution for those who want to invest but don't want their money going toward companies they feel engage in unethical practices. You can learn more about ethical and impact investing in chapter 10.

CAN'T I JUST DO IT MYSELF?

"Hold up, you mentioned in the last section that the robo-advisor would be investing me in Vanguard, Fidelity, BlackRock, Schwab, and the like," you might be thinking. "Couldn't I just cut out the middle man and do it myself?"

Yes, you could. But even though you could, it doesn't mean either that you should or that you'll want to take on the task of being a DIY investor.

"Do-it-yourself can work when you're ready to learn a bunch about what you should be doing, are ready to spend the time to execute that, and are ready to learn about what messes people up as humans looking at the behavioral finance side of it," says Benke. "You may know you have to pick three funds across broad categories, rebalance at least once a year, and make sure you're saving enough generally, but do you always rebalance? Do you look at the market before you rebalance? Do you look at fund level performance and try to decide if you should've picked that Vanguard Total International Fund or maybe now you should switch to the Schwab Total International Fund? There are a lot of factors that still come into play, even though people try to boil down the overall index fund strategy as simple and easy enough to do it yourself."

IS IT SAFE TO USE A ROBO-ADVISOR?

"Definitely safe as long as the firm is SEC and FINRA registered and has SIPC insurance, which all the firms are basically required to have," says Benke. "The common worry is that the firm is newer and will fold, and then what happens to my money? It's different than a bank folding, because you'll get the shares back and just have to put them in another, less fancy account. If the firm went out of business but you're the beneficial owner of those shares, you would just in-kind transfer out."

Benke also acknowledges that higher-net-worth individuals sometimes express concern over another Bernie Madoff situation resulting from investing with a robo-advisor. Bernie Madoff is a former investment advisor who ran the biggest Ponzi scheme in Wall Street history, which lost his clients billions of dollars. The fear is that when a robo-advisor tells you that you have X amount of money invested, how can you be certain the money is actually there?

The fallout from the Madoff Ponzi scheme really did change regulations in the financial world. "We're required to have third-party auditors that come in and check that the money that we have for our customers is actually what we say we have," says Benke. "These surprise audits happen at least annually, and they're on record at the SEC, so clients can go and download the results."

THE PERKS AND PITFALLS OF USING A ROBO-ADVISOR

As with all investment choices, there are both pros and cons to using a robo-advisor.

Perks
Tax-Loss Harvesting
The term *tax-loss harvesting* gets thrown around a lot when you're looking at robo-advisors. It's a big selling point for why you should use a robo-advisor, but what the heck does it mean?

"Since investments that you hold can go up and down, we hold different kinds of them to diversify them together," explains Benke. "When they go down, the IRS has a bonus for you where you can save taxes by effectively taking a deduction for losses. The way you take that deduction is you have to sell the investment. The trick is that you don't want to be uninvested, either. So, when you sell the investment, you also want to buy back [a similar investment] to ensure you keep your portfolio in shape. So, tax-loss harvesting is just a fancy term for looking for losses and taking the deduction to save you taxes."

It makes sense why robo-advisors tout their practice of tax-loss harvesting as an advantage, because you won't want to spend your time scouring your investments for tax-loss harvesting opportunities if you're a DIY investor.

Rebalancing

"Emotion is something we want to get rid of," says Nugent. "We believe over time, markets will revert back to the mean. So, let's look at the history of the US markets—the S&P 500 returns 7 to 9 percent on average. The problem is 'average' never actually happens. It's usually higher returns and lower returns. If you're getting double-digit returns, history would say that at some point you're bound for a correction and a reversion to the mean. The same thing happens on the downside. If the market is negative for a bunch of years, history would show that at some point, people are going to look at it and say, 'Things are on sale, and we're going to go buy some.'

"But in the moment, when you look at all the headlines, they're usually scary on the downside or really exciting on [the] upside. People typically don't rebalance. What you end up seeing is people will hold their losers for far longer than they should and sell their winners prematurely. The idea is to systematize the logic around rebalancing and always be disciplined around when you're going to trim off something and buy more of something else. So, we automate that process for our clients."

Protecting Your Portfolio from You

Remember risk tolerance back in chapter 3 and how it's important to protect your portfolio from yourself? Well, robo-advisors provide a buffer between you and your investments. Granted, you can always get in there and tinker with and even liquidate your investments if you're really panicking during a market correction, but maybe using a robo-advisor will be enough to prevent you from getting hyper-emotional when seeing a dip in the market.

Pitfalls

Fees

You're going to be paying a fee if you want any level of customized financial advice. That's completely reasonable. Fees themselves are not the issue. The issue is whether you're actually getting the value you should for the fee you're paying. Not all robo-advisors are created equal, so it's up to you to do the due diligence and determine if your fee is worth the value you're getting.

Personalization, to a Point

Unless you're coming to the table with at least one significant comma ($100,000), you'll likely get a rather generic version of personalized finance, with calculators and algorithms building a portfolio based on the questions you answer when you sign up. Robo-advisors will continue to evolve and tweak offerings, but it's not far-fetched to think you'll need at least $100,000 to get higher-quality service with more customization. Double commas will get you much more attention!

You Like Being Really Hands-On

You just may be a natural DIY person, and that's okay. You certainly can be hands-on with your robo-advisor if you want, but it does come back to that question of value. Why are you paying the fee, then?

You Want a Long-Term Relationship

"We're big believers in being able to speak to someone who is qualified," says Nugent. "But I don't think it's something that necessarily needs to be done on a full-time basis, at least for the average person."

Many robo-advisors do provide access to financial advisors and, in some cases, CFPs, but the latter usually depends on your assets.

"What if you have a good advisor over the phone, but they get promoted or leave?" poses Douglas A. Boneparth at Bone Fide Wealth. "Maybe you poured your life situation out to Jim, and then call later to find out that Jim has been replaced by Kim. Jim took terrible notes, and now you have to start all over with Kim."

While many robo-advisors do provide humans to give you financial advice, it doesn't always mean developing a long-term relationship with an advisor. While you could also lose a financial advisor at a traditional brokerage firm, too, they often are better at coordinating a hand-off because you've had a long-term relationship with one specific person.

WHEN ARE YOU READY TO USE A ROBO-ADVISOR?

The typical Betterment customer, according to Benke, is around thirty-seven years old, is getting further along in a career, and earns around $100,000. His or her financial situation may be starting to get a little more complex, so he or she decides to outsource instead of going the DIY route.

Nugent describes a typical Wealthsimple customer profile in a similar manner. "[They are] very, very concentrated on their career and doesn't have time necessarily to do this themselves or, frankly, maybe doesn't trust themselves to do it themselves."

However, you don't have to be a "typical customer" in order to start. Since there is a plethora of robo-advisors with no minimum account balances required, the door is open for you to take advantage before you're well established in your career or have a high net worth. You just need to be sure to have checked off all the boxes in chapter 1 indicating that you're in a financially healthy position before you start investing. Or, you can also turn to a robo-advisor to help with retirement planning, especially if you don't have an employer-sponsored plan.

"Any investor who has any sort of meaningful debt should pay that off," says Nugent. "Someone needs to have the right time horizon. We say at Wealthsimple, if you're investing for less than three years, you need to maybe just look at something that's guaranteed like a cash equivalent. We want people thinking long-term because what happens month-to-month and year-to-year is unpredictable."

As always, be sure you do the math on fees before you start. You want to be able to invest enough that the benefit outweighs the cost of using a robo-advisor.

THE BROKERAGE I ALREADY USE OFFERS A ROBO-ADVISOR

Not to be one-upped, many brokerage firms have started to offer their own versions of a robo-advisor. Vanguard, Fidelity, and Charles Schwab are all examples of well-established brokerage firms that have launched robo-advisors with varying levels of functionality and capability.

However, just because the company you've been using to do your ETF or index fund investing offers a robo-advisor tool doesn't mean it's the one you should use.

It comes back to what you want from your robo-advisor and how it's adding value. In some cases, you may find that it makes sense to level up from investing solo to getting customized advice from a company you already trust. In other cases, you might look under the hood and see that the brokerage just slapped together a robo-advisor option to compete in the marketplace and try to attract more Millennials to its services. Another consideration: you're likely to only be investing in that brokerage's funds. Going to a robo-advisor like Betterment, Wealthsimple, or Wealthfront means they're looking for the lowest-cost funds at all the major brokerages.

Again, I'm not saying it's a hard no. You just need to do your due diligence to decide if it's actually best for you and makes your life easier.

IS IT TIME TO SPEAK TO A HUMAN?

Technology can only take you so far, and eventually it just may be time for you to speak to a human.

You should speak to an advisor "whenever you have questions you can't answer or need confirmation," advises Benke. "There's also another end, which is if there's a lot of complexity. You have many different types of financial goals, also you own a house, you work in two states, you have lots of kid-related expenses from day to day to long-term saving for college, your tax situation is complicated with different deductions, dependent care, transit, maybe a small business on the side. There are lots of things that make the picture more complicated and make it even more compelling to talk to somebody."

In some cases, you can reach a human via your robo-advisor, but you may also have concluded that you'd prefer an ongoing personal relationship with a financial advisor. If that's the right fit for you, then here's what you should know.

What You Need to Know About an Advisor

- Does he/she uphold fiduciary or suitability standards?
  - Fiduciary means your advisor does what's in your best interest, not just what is suitable.

- How does your advisor get paid?
  - Fee-only simplifies the relationship. If your advisor takes a commission, you should know when and if that impacts what he or she puts in your portfolio.

- What are your advisor's credentials?
  - A CFP, or certified financial planner, is really the gold standard, but not a requirement. If your financial advisor is not a CFP, you should still ensure he or she is a fiduciary and ask about credentials and experience.

You Need to Feel Comfortable

"Go into that first conversation understanding it might not work out that first go-around," says Kelly Lannan, director, Fidelity Investments. "Go in with the highest hopes, but at the same time, know that it might not stick and you have to be okay with that. You have to go in with specific questions in mind. You have to be very honest about your situation. After the fact, reflect on that conversation and ask yourself if this is the person to help you or do you want to speak to someone else."

WHERE TO SPEAK TO A HUMAN

Want a human advisor but worried about being rejected based on your small stack of cash? Don't worry, size doesn't matter to all advisors. Here are some resources for you to consider if you want to hire a financial advisor:

XY Planning Network: XYPN is an organization of fee-only financial advisors specifically focused on Generation X and Generation Y clients. Advisors are required to be both CFPs and fiduciary advisors, which helps reduce the research you need to do. There are no asset minimum requirements, and some advisors offer a monthly retainer service. You can also reach your advisor virtually. You can learn more at XYPlanningNetwork.com.

Garrett Planning Network: Garrett offers clients access to a network of fee-only, fiduciary CFP professionals. Members of the network do not accept commissions or any other compensation directly from clients. There are no income or asset minimums to become a client, and many offer one-off meetings by the hour if you're looking for help on a specific issue instead of a long-term relationship. You can learn more at garrettplanningnetwork.com.

National Association of Personal Financial Advisors: NAPFA is another way to find fee-only, fiduciary CFPs; however, some NAPFA advisors have asset minimums for clients, as the organization has no rule dictating that they can't. You can learn more at napfa.org.

Ask a friend: Try your own network of friends and family to see if they have any recommendations for a financial advisor. There is one caveat here. You may not want to use the same financial advisor as your bestie or your parents or siblings. It could be akin to using the same therapist. Obviously, they shouldn't be sharing your personal information, but it might just feel a tiny bit awkward.

ARE ROBO-ADVISORS AND HUMAN ADVISORS MUTUALLY EXCLUSIVE?

There's nothing wrong with taking advantage of both worlds.

"People have a need for advice when they need it on their own terms," says Nugent, a former wealth services provider himself. "Whether that's through video chat, the phone, text message, email, or in person, everyone has a different kind of style. If you're going through some sort of life event, it's complicated. It's not always black and white. Technology is really good at solving the black-and-white challenges that exist, but the ability to speak to someone human provides a different perspective that makes you think about other things that might be happening."

Using a robo-advisor now might be the best way for you to enter the market, invest consistently, protect your portfolio from your own meddling hands, and still get some human advice along the way. Then, as your life and financial needs change, perhaps you end up pivoting to working with a human advisor. But even that doesn't mean transferring all your assets away from your robo-advisor and over to a human. You can still do both if you prefer. Remember: it depends!

CHECKLIST FOR WHETHER A ROBO-ADVISOR IS RIGHT FOR YOU

❑ You're ready to start investing in the first place!

   • Have you "earned the right to invest," as Boneparth says? Go back to chapter 1 and make sure.

❑ Your financial situation isn't too complicated.

- As Benke mentioned, there are times when it makes sense to hire a dedicated professional to ensure you're minimizing the taxes and maximizing the profits on your investments.

❑ You want help.

- It's okay if you want to be a completely hands-on DIY investor. But if you want help with asset allocation, rebalancing, tax-loss harvesting, and even determining your risk tolerance, then a robo-advisor could be a good fit.

❑ Do you need or want a long-term relationship with a person?

- A robo-advisor may offer access to financial professionals, but not always in a one-on-one capacity to develop a long-term relationship. If that's important to you, then ask your robo-advisor if it's possible to develop such a relationship, or consider just hiring a human advisor instead.

Chapter 10

Impact Investing— Making Money Without Compromising Your Ethics or Religious Beliefs

OTHER THAN WHEN I saw the cult classic movie *Wall Street*, I didn't give the idea of ethical investing too much thought in my early twenties. I also wasn't actually investing, so it didn't necessarily need to be a thought yet. Then a serendipitous conversation enlightened me on how an activist viewed the stock market.

I was sipping iced tea while sitting in a rocking chair on a screen porch in Georgia. It was exactly as quaint as it sounds. A rock-and-roll musician, his wife, and the major network news reporter I was shadowing were talking about conservation and other environmental issues. The reporter and I were there on assignment to interview the musician about his tree farm, so the progression to discussing general environmental issues made sense.

The BP Deepwater Horizon oil spill had occurred just a few months prior, so the news had been strewn with images of the damage done to the surrounding beaches and wetlands and of animals being killed or displaced.

Suddenly, the musician's voice hardened. "Can you believe people are investing in BP now and making money off this horrific event?" he posed to the group.

This got my attention.

I'd spent a lot of that summer teaching myself about how to best handle my money after graduating college in a year, but I'd yet to consider the ethical side of the equation.

One sentence shifted the way I viewed investing. At what cost do you plan to earn and build your wealth? We collectively rail against outsourcing to countries with weak labor laws and get outraged over the systemic, horrifying behaviors of a CEO—and yet many of us still continue to invest in companies that financially benefit from the practices we claim to stand against. In return, we, the investors, benefit.

In many ways, you can be in control of where your money goes as an investor.

ARE YOUR INVESTMENTS REALLY LIVING UP TO YOUR STANDARDS?

Unfortunately, investing in a fund, whether it's a mutual fund, index fund, or ETF, can mean you're financially supporting and benefiting from a company that partakes in practices you morally or philosophically oppose. It could be that you disagree with the company's environmental policies or that it builds a product you don't support or that it's had a history of poor labor practices. When you invest in a broad index, you can't opt out of investing in specific companies with which you disagree.

The S&P 500 index includes casinos, and alcohol, oil, and pharmaceutical companies. That may not bug you, and it's perfectly okay that it doesn't, but there are those who want to invest in a way that aligns with their values. Buying ETFs and mutual funds without doing thorough research could mean that your money is tied up with something you find unsavory at best and downright unethical or harmful at worst.

WHAT IS IMPACT INVESTING?

"Impact investing, by definition, says that a company has to be earning revenue that is aligned with one of the UN Sustainable Development Goals," says Dave Fanger, CEO and founder of Swell, an impact investing platform. "That's an important distinction [from] some of the [other kinds of investing] you hear about, like ESG [environmental, social, and governance] or SRI [socially responsible investing], which is really more of a broad umbrella term."

What Are the UN Sustainable Development Goals?

"Goals that laid out the groundwork for businesses, non-businesses, and world leaders to follow and get behind that address things like climate change and energy efficiency," says Fanger. "These are goals that reach out to 2030 and beyond, trying to address major social and environmental issues."

The seventeen goals defined by the UN[1] are:

1. No poverty
2. Zero hunger
3. Good health and well-being
4. Quality education
5. Gender equality
6. Clean water and sanitation
7. Affordable and clean energy
8. Decent work and economic growth
9. Industry, innovation and infrastructure
10. Reduced inequality
11. Sustainable cities and communities
12. Responsible consumption and production
13. Climate action
14. Life below water
15. Life on land

16. Peace, justice and strong institutions
17. Partnerships to achieve the goals

You can learn more about the specifics of these goals at undp.org.

WHAT IS SOCIALLY RESPONSIBLE INVESTING?

Socially responsible investing, or SRI, isn't quite as strict as impact investing, which vets funds in portfolios with a more critical eye than an SRI portfolio would. It's not unlike the difference between fiduciary and suitability. Impact investing is akin to fiduciary, and therefore looking for the best possible option; while SRI is more like suitability. It's not harmful, but you can probably do better.

ESG (environmental, social, and governance) compliance is often at the center of SRI portfolios. The problem is it's not terribly difficult to obtain ESG compliance, as the bar can be set rather low.

"If you think about it on a spectrum, on one side you'd find things like ethical investing or things that would be negative screening," explains Fanger. "For example, let's remove anything related to tobacco. Then you've got ESG in the middle, where you're saying, 'Let's just find the companies that have good environmental, social, and governance policies.' There are companies out there with ESG ratings that are quite high, but they could be in the oil sector. So, I think you go then to [the other end of the spectrum], and that's where you'll find impact investing. That's saying, 'Not only do we want to see a very high ESG rating, but let's only look at the companies that align with the UN Sustainable Development Goals.' That will then remove a number of questionable businesses that might be efficient with energy usage or water usage, but other companies are creating products that align with green tech or energy efficiency."

HOW TO CHECK UNDER A COMPANY'S HOOD

As a company, Swell specifically looks at its evaluated holdings daily to ensure they remain compliant with the company's standards by using Morgan Stanley Capital International's (MSCI) ESG ratings, which rate companies on a scale from AAA to CCC. Fanger points to a company like Tesla as having a AAA rating, while a Wells Fargo or Volkswagen* would receive a CCC. You and I don't have that kind of time or access to the same types of tools to evaluate these on our own. You can turn to companies like Swell or select SRI- and ESG-compliant mutual funds or ETFs from your brokerage of choice. However, that doesn't always mean you're getting the crème de la crème of companies.

"It's kind of like organic food when it first came out," says Fanger. "Everybody labeled it 'organic,' and then you started looking a little bit closer at those ingredients and thought, 'Uhh, maybe this isn't what I thought.' Same thing here with 'socially responsible' or 'impact investing.' Some of these funds will state what the ESG rating is from MSCI, and you're looking for something that's double B and above†—that's a good, strong indicator of the overall policies and procedures of a company. And then from there you would really look in the prospectus to see if it mentions anything about the revenue they make around the Sustainable Development Goals."

Companies can also pass ESG compliance without passing your own personal gut check. Casinos can be considered ESG compliant through the use of solar panels, but maybe you don't want to invest in one because you disagree with gambling.

You can look up the "holdings" (i.e., the companies included) in a particular fund. For example, Morningstar typically gives free access to

---

*Volkswagen had a major emissions scandal that broke in 2015 while Wells Fargo had a series of scandals from 2016 to 2017, including account fraud and employee mistreatment.

†That means you want to see an ESG rating of BB, BBB, A, AA, or AAA.

the top ten to twenty-five holdings in a particular fund. You should also be able to look up all the holdings through a monthly fund report from your brokerage of choice. If you're having trouble finding it online (because it's not always easy) try actually giving your brokerage a call.

The level to which you want to practice ethical investing, SRI, or impact investing will greatly dictate your approach. Wanting to only invest in SRI-compliant funds that also adhere to the UN Sustainable Development Goals and that have at least a AA ESG rating will result in you needing to do a lot of the heavy lifting with research as well as potentially limiting your diversification and therefore exposing you to more risk. Swell offers investments in 270 companies* meeting the impact investing definition, according to Fanger, but that's only 270 companies. Just the S&P 500 exposes you to 500 large-cap companies in 10 different sectors.

Just because a brokerage firm says a fund is ESG or SRI compliant does not mean it lives up to your standards. If you have a strict code of conduct regarding the type of companies with which you'll do business, you'll need to do more digging.

INVESTING WITH RELIGIOUS BELIEFS IN MIND

Another consideration is a portfolio that only includes companies that align with your religious beliefs. Notably, halal investing is a faith-based approach to picking investments that align with Islamic beliefs. For instance, investing in companies that profit from gambling or produce alcohol, tobacco, or pork products wouldn't comply. That instantly eliminates a lot of common index funds. The S&P 500, for instance, has Molson Coors Brewing Company (alcohol) and MGM Resorts International (gambling).

Having to vet each company in an index is incredibly tedious, so some robo-advisors, like Wealthsimple, have created halal-compliant portfolios.

---

*At the time of our interview.

CAN I STILL MAKE A DECENT RETURN ON MY INVESTMENTS?

One of the biggest concerns by far when it comes to impact investing or placing restrictions on your portfolio due to ethical or religious beliefs is whether you can still receive a healthy return.

"The main thing we deal with is this idea that I'm going to sacrifice returns," says Fanger. "The data is showing otherwise."

One such data point Fanger recommends is the comparison of MSCI's KLD 400 Social Index compared to the S&P 500. The MSCI KLD 400 Social Index started in 1990 and has outperformed the S&P 500, according to Fanger. This isn't leaps and bounds better, more like a few hundred points. However, just because the index overall performed well doesn't mean the returns from those funds always win. You have to look at specifics when you're investing, especially expense ratios.

The expense ratios for SRI funds coming from companies like Vanguard, a company that's generally considered to have low expense ratios, are higher than funds that are not necessarily SRI compliant. For example, in the winter of 2018, Vanguard charged a 0.20 percent expense ratio with a minimum investment of $3,000 for its Vanguard FTSE Social Index Fund Investor Shares (VFTSX). The Vanguard S&P 500 Index Fund Admiral Shares (VFIAX), also with a $3,000 minimum, only charged a 0.04 percent expense ratio. The SRI-compliant fund (VFTSX) didn't have an Admiral shares option, only an Institutional Investor option with a minimum of $5 million and a 0.12 percent expense ratio.

So, yes, you can make a decent return—but the fees might do more harm than those attached to non-SRI-compliant funds. So impact investing exclusively could be financially problematic.

"Keep in mind that as your investing program gets more specialized, you're investing in segments of the market, and that might expose you to a little bit more volatility, for instance, relative to the entire market or the entire global market that holds a lot more securities," says Maria Bruno, CFP®, a senior investment analyst for Vanguard Investment Strategy

Group. The more specialized you become, the more it could reduce your diversification, which exposes you to more risk as you narrow the sectors in which you're willing to invest.

This isn't meant to discourage you from building an impact investing or SRI-compliant portfolio, but you must consider more than just the returns of the index. It's also about the cost of the funds, which impacts your net returns. Adding impact-investing-compliant funds can be a way to diversify your existing portfolio, but investing exclusively in such funds may minimize your diversification and increase your risk.

CHECKLIST FOR IMPACT/SRI INVESTING

❑ Do some research if you want to really ensure your investments aren't tangled up with anything you deem nefarious. Don't take at face value a fund labeled "ESG compliant."

❑ Understand that your standards and the brokerage's standards may be different.

❑ Avoid relying exclusively on impact investing. While you won't necessarily be sacrificing returns, it could leave you without broad diversification and therefore subject to a higher amount of risk.

❑ Adding an SRI- or ESG-compliant fund to your existing portfolio is a smart way to diversify.

Chapter 11

Riding Out the Panic of a Market Crash

I DON'T HAVE a kitschy story for you to start this chapter. That's the disadvantage of writing a book about investing at the tender age of twenty-nine, with only seven years of investing experience. I haven't truly experienced a market crash. Sure, I was alive when the dot-com bubble burst, and I certainly experienced the fallout from the Great Recession, but I wasn't an investor (unless you include amassing impressive Beanie Baby and Pokémon card collections in the late 1990s that grossed negative returns).

Sure, I've weathered a few market corrections since jumping into the fray back in 2012, but honestly, I experienced a really significant bull market for most of my early investing years. The only thing I can tell you is "Winter is coming"—it's still relevant to throw in that reference, right?

A market crash is going to happen during our tenures as investors. At the very least, a bubble will burst or a significant market correction will occur. Whatever we call it, we're likely to face a real crash of some sort. Maybe once, maybe several times. As they say, "What's past is prologue."

There is no way to predict how the stock market will perform during the course of our journey as investors. However, understanding the past may help us ride out the panic of a market correction or even a crash. Okay, that might sound strange to you. Why would reading a horror story make you feel encouraged to invest? Well, because of what happens after: the market recovers. Learning the history of bubbles and crashes helps reinforce the idea that the stock market is indeed cyclical.

A HELPFUL HISTORY LESSON

There are four significant market crashes and two bubbles that rookie investors should know about before getting into the game. Keep in mind, these summaries are significantly simplified versions of what happened because frankly, each crash or bubble could be its own book.

First, You Need a Basic Understanding of What an Index Is

Have you ever watched CNBC, Fox Business, or any business news–specific channel and heard an anchor say something like "The Dow was up 190 points at closing"? Or maybe your parents had the TV on and you just happened to hear such a phrase as white noise in the background. The "Dow Jones Industrial Average," the "S&P 500," the "Nasdaq," "Russell 3000," and many more are all major stock indices.

You may remember my mention of an index when we discussed index funds. An index is a grouping of stocks (or bonds) that is used as a benchmark for market performance. Each index tracks a different grouping of companies. The Dow Jones Industrial Average (DJIA) benchmarks thirty of the most influential companies in the United States. Founded in 1896, it is one of the oldest indices in the world, so naturally, the thirty companies* change over time. There is bound to be overlap among indices. For example, Apple is on the DJIA and also on the S&P 500 index.

The S&P 500 index is another one of the most frequently referenced

---

*It started with only twelve companies.

indices. As the name implies, it tracks five hundred large-cap* US companies from a variety of sectors. The S&P 500 is often used as a benchmark for how the overall stock market is doing.

You will hear references to indices throughout this chapter and your entire investing life. "It's relevant to understand what an index is," says Jill Schlesinger, CFP®, CBS News business analyst and author of *The Dumb Things Smart People Do with Their Money*. "The reason why it becomes important is to understand what you're comparing yourself against. So, do I think it's important to understand the difference between how the Dow is calculated versus the way the S&P 500 is calculated? Not really. What's important to know is that there are different indexes, and the reason we talk about them is to give us a means to compare ourselves against a specific index."

Another important term to understand throughout this chapter is *recession*. It refers to a period of stagnant or even declining economic growth. Some of the indicators used to determine if the country is in a recession include unemployment, industrial production, trade, and oil consumption.

Okay, with that tidbit out of the way, let's go back in time to examine some peaks and valleys in the stock market.

Tulip Mania

This isn't a stock market crash, but one of the most commonly discussed examples of a bubble. Bubbles, as described in chapter 2, follow a simple pattern: a commodity becomes popular; people go crazy trying to buy it, thinking someone else will pay even more; the price of said commodity

---

Large-cap refers to companies that are valued at more than $5 billion. This value is determined by something called market capitalization. Market capitalization is (stock price) × (number of shares issued). For example, let's say Joey's Donuts issued 500,000 shares to investors, and each share is worth $130. Joey's Donuts' market capitalization would then be ($130) × (500,000) = $65,000,000. Large-cap companies are usually seen as stable and, dare I say, safer investments because their sheer size makes them less likely to go under. While not entirely true, the phrase "too big to fail" comes to mind.

hits a peak; people start selling; panic sets in; and the whole market around the commodity plummets.

What Happened

Hundreds of years ago, the Dutch got so crazy for tulip bulbs that it created a scarcity, and thus supply and demand drove the price of tulip bulbs up and up. Folks dumped their life savings and traded land to stockpile bulbs. Ultimately, as with all bubbles, it burst in 1637. People started to sell the stockpiled bulbs in order to actually cash in on their investments, which led to more and more people selling, which made prices plummet, which only made more people panic and try to sell, which triggered a crash.

Black Tuesday, October 29, 1929

What Happened

The stock market crash of October 1929 precipitated the Great Depression. After a bull market during the 1920s, many stocks were overvalued due to speculation. But the American economy was already showing signs of a decline. Unemployment had risen, wages were low, large bank loans couldn't be liquidated, and steel production was declining.

The stock prices started to fall in September through early October, which triggered panic from investors. Some historians point to the Hatry Crisis as a contributing factor. Clarence Charles Hatry issued fake securities to investors, a fraud that panicked the UK markets and then impacted the US markets because investors pulled money out to settle the losses they'd experienced from Hatry. The fraud spooked investors, making some wary of continuing to put money into the market. It didn't help that the newspapers of the day were running inflammatory headlines about the widespread panic.

The crash began on October 24, 1929. The final day of the crash, October 29, 1929, is known now as Black Tuesday. Fourteen billion dollars[1] were lost on that day alone, with the entire four days seeing losses of $30 billion. That's more than $400 billion in 2018 dollars. By 1932, investments were worth only 20 percent of what they'd been worth pre-crash in 1929.

During this market crash, there were also runs on banks, which you may remember if you've ever seen the movie *It's a Wonderful Life*. Panicked Americans ran to their local bank in an effort to take out their life savings for safekeeping at home. The banks didn't have enough money in the vaults to satisfy the demand, and many closed. Some would reopen and offer customers a fraction of what they'd actually saved, but others shuttered entirely,[2] which naturally caused more panic.

The runs on the bank sparked the creation of the Federal Deposit Insurance Corporation (FDIC). Your FDIC-insured bank today now provides protection of up to $250,000 in cash, as of 2018. If anything were to happen to your bank, you'd get your money back up to $250,000, which is a move to protect the public's confidence in the banking system.

Recovery

The market's recovery depends on how you evaluate the data. Generally, you'll read that it took a whopping twenty-five years for the markets to completely bounce back to pre-crash levels. Bear in mind, the United States did fight World War II during that time period as well.

However, other stock market analysts would argue that it took much less time for the market to actually recover. For one, the twenty-five-year argument doesn't account for the fact that, during the Great Depression, the country was in a period of deflation, and it depends on if you're segmenting the market by indices or looking at the stock market as a whole. Those who make this argument contend the average investor who put a lump sum into an average stock in 1929 right before the crash would've actually ended up breaking even by 1936,[3] assuming they didn't sell their investments when the market crashed.

Black Monday, October 19, 1987

What Happened

Well, clearly we aren't ones for clever new nicknames when dubbing stock market panics. Black Monday occurred nearly sixty years after Black Tuesday. On Monday, October 19, 1987 (Sunday in the United States, as the markets were opening in Asia), a crash started in Hong Kong and spread through the European markets before hitting the United States. This crash showed just how interconnected the global markets had become. However, we can't point fingers at the Asian markets and say it was completely triggered there. Indicators had started to crop up in the United States that a market correction was coming.

The market had been on a bull run that year, with the Dow Jones Industrial Average (DJIA) up 44 percent in a matter of seven months, reaching a high of 2,722 points in August. That fact alone set off some alarm bells that a market correction could be on the horizon. Then the federal government announced a trade deficit that was higher than expected, which caused the dollar to lose value. The creation of portfolio insurance fostered a false sense of security, and forced selling to protect portfolios once the crash started. Plus, computer technology in the form of program trading to place large-scale buy or sell orders was relatively new to the market and served as a bit of a scapegoat after the crash.

On Friday, October 16, the DJIA dropped 108.35 points.[4] It was the first time in history the Dow had ever lost 100 points in one day and was the most significant drop since the Great Depression. For today's context, 100 points is no longer considered a significant drop because of how high the DJIA has climbed since the 1980s. For example, the Dow lost more than 1,000 points in a market correction in early 2018 that didn't create widespread panic.

Then, on Monday, October 19, after investors saw what had happened in the Asian and European markets, people started to sell. The Dow opened at 2,246.73 and then plummeted as soon as the opening bell rang. It dropped 508.32 points, to 1,738.41, by day's end, a 22.6 percent loss, making the previous Friday's historic drop look like chump change.

Recovery
The recovery process started almost immediately. The Dow actually bounced back 300 points within just two days and had returned to pre-crash highs in two years.

Dot-com Bubble and Crash of 2000–2002

What Happened

The dot-com bubble burst when I was only in the fifth grade, but it's such a touchstone for modern investing that I still know some of the cracks made about companies like Pets.com, and I actually remember using Ask Jeeves. For you younger Millennials and Gen Zers, that was Google before Google. Jeeves was a butler on the website to whom you directed your burning questions. We could be still saying "Ask Jeeves" instead of "Google it" or "Ask Siri/Alexa" today if things went differently.

The late 1990s saw a huge uptick in tech-related IPOs (initial public offerings). The internet was still in its early years and the potential for a "new economy" led to wild speculation. As with all bubbles, tech companies were overvalued and given millions in funding from investors all hoping to find the next big thing.

Pets.com still serves as a cautionary tale: it went from an IPO to being liquidated as a company in less than a year. The day of the IPO, in February 2000, Pets.com stock sold for $11 a share, and by November 2000, the share price had dropped to $0.19.

While other crashes featured the Dow Jones Industrial Average as the benchmark measuring the stock market's performance, this crash focuses on the Nasdaq Composite Index. Nasdaq started in 1971 as the world's first electronic stock exchange, so it should be no surprise that a lot of tech companies choose to go public on the Nasdaq stock exchange. While not exclusively a technology-focused index, it heavily leans toward tech companies. For that reason, the Nasdaq is often used as the barometer instead of the Dow Jones when discussing the dot-com bubble.

The Nasdaq exploded with growth in the late 1990s, with all the tech company IPOs moving from around 1,000 points in 1995 to more than 5,000 in 2000. The peak of the bubble occurred when the Nasdaq reached an all-time high of 5,046.86 on March 10, 2000. On March 11, 2000, the bubble burst, and the Nasdaq started to drop. By the fall of 2002, it had dropped as low as a little over 1,100 points.[5] Its previous high wasn't surpassed until almost exactly fifteen years later, in April 2015.

The tech bubble bursting wasn't the only event to drastically impact the stock market and the recession of the early 2000s. The 9/11 terrorist attacks also sent shock waves around the global markets. The New York Stock Exchange and Nasdaq closed for four days following the attacks, to prevent panic selling by investors. When trading resumed, the market experienced a 7.1 percent decline in one day. The Dow Jones was down 14 percent overall by the end of the week, with the S&P 500 down 11.6 percent.

Recovery

The Nasdaq, Dow Jones, and S&P 500 all returned to pre-9/11 prices within one month of the attacks, but the market did dip again in the latter half of 2002. By 2003, the market appeared to be back on an upward trajectory—an upward trajectory that would fumble just five years later.

The Great Recession, 2007–2009

What Happened

The Great Recession is the market crash often cited as the reason Millennials don't get into the investing game. We came of age during the crisis and not only saw but experienced the fallout firsthand when we attempted to enter the job market.

The subprime mortgage crisis typically takes the heat as the culprit for the Great Recession. Home buyers were approved for mortgages for which they weren't qualified, because of either poor credit or low income. These subprime loans were often positioned to buyers as cheap at first, and then would bloat with higher interest rates and monthly payments after the first couple of years.

The buyers would sometimes be sold on the message that within two years they could clean up their credit and just refinance the subprime mortgage to get a better deal and avoid the inflated interest rate. Obviously, that's not what happened, and people soon were faced with horribly high monthly payments that made no dent in the actual principal of their mortgage balance, even after a few years of payments. This was also exacerbated by the fact that some people took out mortgages without any money down, so the entire home was financed with a loan.

The banks knew these loans were high risk. Sometimes these mortgages were bundled together as "mortgage-backed securities" and sold as investments to financial institutions, where they could end up in pension funds and mutual funds.

Everything started to go sideways when the Federal Home Loan Mortgage Corporation (Freddie Mac) announced that it would no longer purchase subprime mortgages or mortgage-backed securities. Within a few months, New Century Financial Corporation and American Home Mortgage Investment Corporation declared bankruptcy. Investments that were backed by subprime mortgages were now viewed as risky, and housing prices began to fall across the country. This is what started to impact the everyday American. As house prices fell, people suddenly went "upside down" on their mortgages, which meant they owed more than the house was now worth.

The next hit came as the stock market began to decline. The Dow alone went from more than 14,000 points to 6,547 in only one and a half years. That resulted in a huge blow to retirement plans, pensions, and the portfolios of average Americans.

As this was all happening, investment banks that were bullish on their investments in subprime mortgages began to collapse. First was Bear Stearns, in March 2008, followed by Lehman Brothers declaring bankruptcy that September. The federal government stepped in, offering relief (financed by the taxpayer) to struggling financial institutions, banks, and even some automakers. You may remember that the expression "too big to fail" became quite popular at this time.

Recovery

The summer of 2009 is often cited as the end of the Great Recession because the stock market began to rebound and unemployment rates began to go down. The government created the Dodd-Frank Wall Street Reform and Consumer Protection Act in the aftermath of the Great Recession to more strictly regulate the financial industry, but as political factions change in the White House, so, too, do regulations on financial institutions.

While 2009 marked the end of the Great Recession on paper, the fallout for the average American was far from over. It took far longer for the job market to heat back up, and many Americans were dealing with foreclosed homes, trashed credit scores, and decimated investment portfolios.

The stock market, however, went on a bull run. Investors who stayed the course during the Great Recession were well rewarded in the decade following the crash. The Dow had dropped to 6,547 points in 2009, but it soared to new, prerecession highs by 2018, when it closed at more than 26,000 points. The S&P 500 index quadrupled during the bull run, from its low of 676 points in March 2009 to as high as 2,872 points in January 2018.[6]

PLAYBOOK FOR HANDLING A DOWNTURN

It's stressful to watch your net worth suddenly drop by hundreds or thousands or much, much more in just a day. Unfortunately, that's what happens when the market tumbles, crashes, plummets, drops, takes a bath, dips, or whichever other term you prefer. Your primary job is to leave well enough alone. But that can be hard, so here are some tips on how to handle the anxiety in the pit of your stomach.

First, Know It's Coming—Eventually

I've said it many times already in this book, and I'm going to keep pushing this point because it's important. The market will go down.

"What goes up must come down. That's a theory in all aspects of life, and that is what's going to happen to the market," says Kelly Lannan, director, Fidelity Investments. "Can we tell when the market is going to go down? No, we cannot do that, and if we tried to time it, we'd drive ourselves crazy and miss out on a lot of opportunities."

Be Wary of Dramatic Headlines

"Worst Decline in History!" and other flashy headlines may be excellent clickbait, but they're terrible for the novice investor's constitution. Besides, such headlines provide little to no context. We saw a few market corrections in 2018. It was easy for news outlets to vie for your eyeballs by writing things like "The Biggest Point Decline in History!" While true, the statement didn't provide context that the Dow Jones Industrial Average had set a highest closing record at 26,616.71 on January 26, 2018.[7] So, when it "went into free fall" and "plunged" (words actually used in articles) the following week, it was still higher than it had been just five weeks prior, in December 2017.

Know What's Going On in the World

The market reacts to what's happening both nationally and globally. The day after the United Kingdom voted to leave the European Union, a vote more commonly known as Brexit, it wasn't just the UK market that soured; our stock market had a dip as well. Generally, any sort of uncertainty will disrupt the market at least a little bit because people get nervous.

Just Wait a Day

If the market does start to take a tumble, consider waiting a day, advises Colleen Jaconetti, CFP®, senior investment analyst for Vanguard Investment Strategy Group. "Just try to think through 'Why am I going to do this?' because the hard part is you have to make three decisions: when to get out, when to get back in, and where to invest in the meantime. Getting all three of those right can be very difficult."

Turn to the Past for Comfort

It may seem crazy that I've just spent several pages overviewing awful times in the market, but hopefully that knowledge will actually help you weather the storm of a market crisis. Remember the opening story of this book, when my dad explained to me that the market is a cyclical beast?

Lannan also advises taking a different approach, especially if pure storytelling doesn't help you. "Looking at visuals over time and charts—especially if you're a visual person—you can actually see what can happen to your money, even through downturns."

Speak to Someone

Get your advisor on the phone, if you have one, or even just talk to someone you know with some investing experience, whether that's a peer, parent, or coworker. Preferably go to someone with a higher risk tolerance than you, who isn't going to Chicken Little the situation and recommend that you "Sell, sell, sell!" or "Stuff all your cash in a safe and never invest again!" It's never a bad move to speak to a seasoned investor who has actually weathered some of the more significant bubbles or market crashes over the years.

Honestly, Just Don't Look at Your Portfolio

"I have to tell you, through the financial market crisis [of 2008], I didn't open my statement at all," admits Jaconetti. "I knew I wasn't going to like it, I wasn't going to be happy with it."

It's okay to be informed, to know what's going on, she says, but that doesn't mean you need to look at your portfolio and see the temporary damage being done.

Stick to Your Plan

One reason Jaconetti didn't need to look at her portfolio is because she'd put a plan in place and knew how important it was to stick to it. "People who did get out [during the 2008 financial crisis]—it took them years to recover," says Jaconetti. "If you got out of the market and went all to bonds or all to cash, the break-even was more than five years. If you're getting out at the bottom or close to the bottom, you don't know when to get back in. If you didn't get back in as it was going up, and it just kept going up, you missed a very significant bull market after that. Hindsight is always 20/20. No one knew when it was going to hit the bottom or turn around, so really have a long-term focus. The more important thing: have the right asset allocation, be diversified, have low-cost funds, and then try to tune out the noise, knowing you have a plan."

Don't Sell . . . Usually

Remember the story in chapter 3 about my professor and her neighbor? The moral of that story was that you don't really make or lose money until you sell. You lock in your losses when you sell. The general advice when you have a well-balanced and diversified portfolio is to not sell. Of course, if you're doing individual stock picking and a company is without a doubt going under, or if you've invested in a highly volatile commodity, that's a slightly different situation.

Remember Your Time Horizon (and That You're Young)

Because this book is written for Millennials, I'm guessing that you're on the younger end of the spectrum. Maybe you're not! But if you have decades until retirement, when you'll need access to some or all your investments, then take solace in the fact that time is on your side.

"The biggest strategy is make sure you understand that you're young," says Lannan. "You can weather the ebbs and flows of the market. Never try to time the market, and just stay consistent with your strategy. When you get closer to certain [milestones], that's the time to rebalance. Don't do it before you need that money because you shouldn't react to anything. Fight against your human nature a little bit."

Consider Investing More, or at Least Leave Your Automatic Contributions Alone

"If your favorite car went on sale, wouldn't you go buy it?" jokes financial education specialist Ashley Fox. "You wouldn't be scared of it. It's just going on sale. If you truly believe the value of that car is worth having, and over time will have greater value than what you paid for it, then by all means, that's the time you rack up."

Granted, a car might not be the most relevant metaphor here, considering that cars depreciate in value, but Fox makes a sound point. It may sound absolutely nutters to you, but you do want to keep on your steady path of investing during a downturn. That is not the time to stop your automatic contributions or take your dividends in cash. (You'll want to reinvest them, if you can.) In fact, some people would even argue that it's a good time to put in a little more.

The logic behind this is that the market is essentially providing you with a fire sale. Stocks are cheap because share prices have gone down, so you get more bang for your buck. It's part of why the system of dollar-cost averaging is highly recommended. If you keep those automatic contributions going, you're buying during a low-cost time, which helps offset your buying in toward the top of the market.

CHECKLIST FOR HANDLING THE PANIC OF A MARKET CRASH

The market is going to go down. It's a fact all investors must face. So, here's what you need to remember when it happens.

❑ Stay calm and remember your investing strategy.

❑ Take some solace in looking at the market's history.

❑ Don't turn off your automatic contributions.

❑ Take a day before making a rash decision.

❑ Check in with a trusted friend, mentor, or financial advisor.

❑ Seriously, just avoid looking at your portfolio.

Chapter 12

Sniffing Out a Scam

READING OVER COMMENTS from my editor, I noticed a question buried within the text: "Does he really pay this much for a life insurance policy? That seems like too much."

The question was about my then boyfriend, now husband, Peach. At the time, he was paying around $50 per month on his $50,000 life insurance policy. This was something I didn't know about until I wrote an article detailing why it's important for people with cosigned private student loan debt to carry life insurance. (Answer: because if your lender doesn't discharge the debt upon death, the cosigner will suddenly need to pay it off and may not have the funds to do so.)

I'd told Peach a few months prior that he really should have a life insurance policy, since his parents had cosigned on some of his student loan debt. It wasn't a long conversation by any means, and I didn't even know he'd been proactive about getting himself a policy until a few months later, when he mentioned paying for it. I didn't ask any questions about where he'd gone or the type of policy he'd picked.

Smash-cut back to me reading my editor's comment.

I started mulling over his point. Why was a twenty-five-year-old with no health issues paying $50 per month for a simple life insurance policy?

So, I asked Peach. "Hey, what kind of life insurance policy do you have?"

Then I got the answer I feared: whole life.

"Oh, how come you picked whole life insurance?"

"I don't know," he said. "I googled 'How to get a life insurance policy' and ended up on the insurance company's website. When I called and explained my situation, the woman on the phone told me that a whole-life insurance policy would be best because some of the money is invested and I get the cash value back. With term life, she said I'd never get money back except if I died, and then my parents would get the payout."

He's right. It is a good sales pitch. It makes sense that lots of people get pushed into a product like whole-life insurance, even when it's not the best fit. For Peach, a whole-life policy made no sense. He didn't have any dependents, wasn't worried about sheltering money from estate taxes, and just wanted some basic coverage in case he died young and his parents were forced to pay off his student loans. A term life insurance policy would've been the perfect fit, about $25 a month cheaper with a larger payout. That's an extra $25 a month that could've been going toward paying off his student loans faster. The problem was that the insurance company rep on the other end of the call probably received a commission when he signed up for a whole-life insurance policy, which means she was incentivized to push him toward one.

After I explained these points, Peach ended up switching his life insurance policy. He nearly tripled his coverage, to $150,000 for a seventy-year term, and saved $25 a month, which meant putting about $300 a year back into his budget. That's an extra student loan payment!

Now, was he scammed? Not exactly. But he also wasn't encouraged to get the financial product that fit him best.

UNFORTUNATELY, a big part of investing is being cautious and developing an excellent bullshit detector. There will always be scams in the marketplace, so let's overview ways to detect a scam, using more than just a gut instinct, and how to properly vet potential investments and advisors.

WHAT THE EXPERTS HAVE TO SAY

With the exception of my first foray into investing (when I called up an advisor at my bank and was sold a particular mutual fund), I've pretty much spent the bulk of my DIY strategy vetting products myself and focusing on low-cost index funds. I've only once purchased an individual stock for the purpose of playing around and learning more about stock picking. I do my best to block out the noise of the hot new stock tip or latest buzzy trend while still keeping myself in the know for the sake of my work and my investing plan.

But I'm human. Of course I'm susceptible to wondering if I should've invested a little money in Bitcoin back when I first started hearing about it, or listened to my gut and bought Netflix stock back at the end of 2011, when shares plummeted, since I was pretty sure the company would stick around. (Yeah, I still kick myself over that one—but I wasn't in a financial position to invest yet.)

I asked the experts for recommendations on how to sniff out a scam in the investing world and for tips on how to realize that a particular company or investment isn't the right fit.

"Keep It Simple, Stupid"

"There are a lot of people who buy stuff because it's sold to them," explains Jill Schlesinger, CFP®, CBS News business analyst and author of *The Dumb Things Smart People Do with Their Money*. "They don't buy it because they understand it. I had a fabulous professor once. He was teaching a big class on options to us young commodities traders, who were trading derivatives. On the blackboard, he wrote in huge letters, 'KISS.' And I thought it was going to be some massive theory about [the] Black-Scholes model, and he's like, 'Keep It Simple, Stupid.' And that's not a bad way to think about your own financial life. If you can't very clearly explain what you just bought, then don't buy it. And look, you know when you're being sold and you know you've got a sixth sense. If there are yellow flags that you're feeling, then don't do it."

"Quick Money" Can Be Code for "Shady"

"Well, *gut check,* I think, is a good word," says Maria Bruno, CFP®, a senior investment analyst for Vanguard Investment Strategy Group. "If it seems too good to be true, then it probably is. So, be careful of gimmicks or strategies that are meant to make quick money, because those are often probably not realistic or just riddled with a lot of shady investment activity."

Choose Advisors/Investments That Share Your Values

"Do your homework on investment providers," says Bruno. "Look at tenured investment firms. Make sure that how that company invests is aligned with your values. You know, a lot of people spend a lot of time thinking about a car and all the work that goes into purchasing the right car. Well, do we as investors spend that much time thinking about what fund we're going to pick? Maybe not, but think it through and understand what you're getting, what you're paying, the tenure of the firm, and the money manager."

Know Your Risk Tolerance

"Take a look at the asset management companies out there," advises Douglas Boneparth, CFP®, founder of Bone Fide Wealth. "These are big names with trillions of dollars. Your BlackRocks, your Vanguards, your Oppenheimers, your Goldman Sachs[es]—they sell mutual funds or

ETFs. Because the space is so commoditized, you're going to be hard pressed to find yourself in a Bernie Madoff situation. You're well covered, the industry is well regulated—you're not going to have a 'burn 'em, cheat 'em, and run' mutual fund or ETF.

"You're going to find products at large institutions that run the gamut from conservative money market funds to relatively risky emerging markets. You'll find funds that are investing in cryptocurrency and private equity companies. We're going well beyond the spectrum of your large US companies.

"But where should you be concerned about sniffing out someone? [Not from the mutual funds or ETFs that the established and regulated asset management companies are offering.] When your buddy comes up to you with a wild idea and wants your cash.

"Financial institutions come to the table with well-regulated products. The consideration is where does that product fall on the risk spectrum, not that you're going to get robbed."

Buy More of What You Already Own

"I don't research the next big tech company," says Ashley Fox, a financial education specialist who started her career working for a Wall Street investment bank. "If I use it, I own it. That's how I invest. I don't go looking for investments. I just buy more of what I own and continue to use. I understand how each company I invest in operates and makes money and what they do."

Were Your Questions Answered?

"There should be an immediate red flag when someone tells you about an investment and you ask questions about it and you're not satisfied with the answer," says Jennifer Barrett, chief education officer for Acorns. "You still don't feel like you understand it. That's my gut check."

Are You Okay with Losing All the Money?

"Even with cryptocurrency, I really researched it for quite a long time before I invested in it," says Barrett. "My personal gut check is I cannot invest in anything unless I at least understand the basic mechanics behind it. With crypto, that means understanding that it's largely a speculative investment and you're betting that someone else is willing to pay more than you. So, how comfortable am I putting money into an investment that has no real intrinsic value, solely on the hope that someone else will pay more? My answer was: I've been watching this for long enough that I can put a little money in, that I'm okay losing with the idea that I might win big. But if I lost everything I invested in it, would it fundamentally affect our ability to reach our goals? How would I feel? Would I be okay if that money just disappeared?"

VETTING FINANCIAL ADVISORS AND PRODUCTS

There are a number of resources out there to help you sort out whether an advisor is sketchy.

BROKER CHECK: The Financial Industry Regulatory Authority (FINRA) offers an online tool that allows you to vet a potential broker/investment advisor. Broker Check allows you to look up a financial advisor by name, Central Registration Depository number, or firm name. This free tool will tell you the number of years the advisor has been active, which exams he or she passed, and the states in which he or she is registered. Most important, it will let you know about any customer complaints, regulatory actions, arbitrations, bankruptcy filings, and criminal or civil judicial proceedings. If your potential (or current) investment advisor or broker isn't registered, it could mean he or she isn't legally allowed to sell securities or offer investment advice.

Find the tool at https://brokercheck.finra.org/.

INVESTMENT ADVISOR PUBLIC DISCLOSURE: The Securities and Exchange Commission (SEC) also provides a free tool for vetting investment advisors. It works in a similar way to FINRA's Broker Check, and also pulls in information from Broker Check. You'll receive details about any disciplinary actions taken against an advisor as well as his or her credentials.

Find the tool at https://www.adviserinfo.sec.gov/.

VERIFY A CFP: The certified financial planner (CFP) designation is the gold standard for financial planners. While financial planners and investment advisors are not always one and the same, you can seek out a CFP who also specializes in investments and estate planning. Should you want to work directly with a CFP, whether for general financial planning or for your investments, you can verify potential candidates through the CFP Board. The tool will tell you if the CFP is indeed certified, whether he or she has a history of disciplinary actions from the CFP Board, and any bankruptcy disclosures in the last decade.

Find the tool at https://www.cfp.net/utility/verify-an-individual -s-cfp-certification-and-background (or type "verify CFP" into a search engine and look for the landing page associated with the CFP Board).

Questions to Ask a Potential Advisor

You should take the time to ask a potential investment advisor questions before doing business.

- What are your experience, certifications, and credentials?
  - There are plenty of certifications and credentials, so the ones you're looking for depend largely on what you want out of an advisor. You'll hear brokers and investment advisors refer to exams such as the Series 7 or Series 63. These licenses are required in order to be able to sell different types

of securities. You can learn more about each one on FINRA's website (http://www.finra.org/industry/qualification-exams).

- Do you uphold the fiduciary standard?
  - The fiduciary standard means the advisor acts in your best interest. Suitability standard means the advisor just has to do only what is suitable for you.
- How do you get paid?
  - As mentioned in chapter 6, commissions, a fee for assets under management, and a flat-rate fee are all ways in which your advisor may get paid. If he or she gets paid a commission, you should know exactly what that means for you and the products in your portfolio.
- How often should I expect to hear from you?
  - At a bare minimum, you should have an annual meeting about your portfolio and goals, but maybe you'd prefer to meet once a quarter or get weekly newsletters or be able to get a response if you're panicking about a market correction. You should be comfortable with the means and frequency of communication that you get from your advisor.
- Will I be working directly with you or also with other people in the firm?
  - It's a bummer to feel as though you have a rapport with someone only to find out that's the pitch person to get your business, and you'll really be dealing with intern Jim down the hall.

Questions to Ask About a Product

You can ask your investment advisor these questions directly, or you can ask them of yourself before you decide to invest in a new product.

- How does this investment work and make me money?
- What is my goal with this investment?

- Is this aligned with my risk tolerance and values?
- How is this helping me reach my (short/medium/long-term) goals?
- Will I be okay if I lose all this money tomorrow?

INVESTMENTS YOU SHOULD QUESTION

First, you should always do your due diligence on any investment, no matter how "safe" it seems.

Second, before you skim this list, it's important for you to understand something. The products you see listed here are not necessarily scams or nefarious products. Some of them make sense for a niche group of people at a particular phase in their lives.

However, many of the products listed below have the potential to be sold to you as smart investments because they pass the suitability test but not the fiduciary one. Some of these investments come with well-crafted sales pitches to make it sound like you'd be a fool to not get in now. You need to do your own research and see if an investment really does fit in your portfolio or if someone is trying to make a commission off you.

Cryptocurrency

"Bitcoin is gambling. If you want to gamble, that's fine," says Sallie Krawcheck, CEO of Ellevest. "Whatever money you put aside to go to Las Vegas, you can use to play around in Bitcoin. At some point, it may become a true asset class, but it is not there yet."

Active Management

Active management, Krawcheck explains, is "the idea of buying and selling funds or stocks through a financial advisor or a broker, or on your own, with the promise of outperforming the market. The research tells us that despite the fact that this has been the value proposition in the industry for the longest period of time, the percent of active managers who consistently outperform over a five-year period is a single-digit percent. By some estimates, it's less than 1 percent. This is a loser's game. This continues in the industry because it makes so very much money from it and because the concept of outperforming is so tantalizing and so compelling."

Whole-Life Insurance

"Buy term, and invest the difference," advises Krawcheck. Whole life comes with steep premiums and fees. If you're unable to pay those premiums, then you could lose some or all of that initial deposited sum. The returns on the invested funds probably aren't great compared to putting the same money in a low-fee index fund. Plus, whole life is just frickin' confusing, and as all the experts have recommended, only buy what you can understand.

Term life is simple, with lower prices, so you get the coverage you need and can invest the difference. Plenty of life insurance agents are happy to sell you a whole-life insurance product, and in fact will probably give you a hard pitch to take it—even if it's not the ideal fit.

Generally, whole-life insurance is recommended for high-net-worth individuals doing everything they can to minimize the impact of estate taxes. For the average Broke Millennial, it's not a fit.

Annuities

"I adore the concept, because if I describe an annuity to anybody, they always say, 'That sounds amazing.' You know, what if [you] could put money in, earn a return, and not outlive your money," says Krawcheck. "Unfortunately, the industry has so overcharged for annuities that [they've] gotten a bad name."

Annuities are one of those products that are easy to build a strong sales pitch for, but that doesn't mean they're a good fit for your financial life and goals. Don't be wowed by a flashy presentation until after you've looked under the hood and investigated the fees and restrictions, and then see if an annuity still fits into your plan.

CHECKLIST FOR SNIFFING OUT SCAMS

❏ After asking all your questions, do you understand what the investment does and how it earns money?

❏ If it's a speculative investment, are you financially and emotionally prepared to lose all the money you invest?

❏ Do you feel like you're being given a sales pitch or does this product make sense with your portfolio's overall goals?

❏ Did you properly vet a broker/financial advisor/investment advisor by asking all the necessary questions and checking the SEC and FINRA databases?

❏ It's cliché, but what's your gut telling you?

Chapter 13

So, You're Ready to Sell an Investment

FOR TWELVE CHAPTERS NOW, we've discussed why you should invest and the ways in which you can. There's been a significant emphasis on the buy-and-hold strategy, but at some point, you're going to want to sell your investments or at least start to take withdrawals from the accounts.

I held on to my first investment for five years before I sold. It was that original mutual fund I opened up via my bank. This wasn't the shrewdest investing decision, especially given its rather high expense ratio, but I left it alone to grow for five years nonetheless.

The right time to sell came a few months before Peach and I got married. Years prior to our engagement, I'd mentally earmarked that mutual fund as a wedding gift to him. Not that I would hand him some sort of paperwork transferring it to his name or anything. No, my idea was to liquidate the fund and use it to make a large payment toward his student loan debt.

You may be wondering why I'd do that after I spent all of chapter 5 waxing poetic about the importance of investing while carrying student loan debt. The logic, for me, was twofold.

1. One of Peach's student loans carried a 7.75 percent interest rate. The math on that just didn't really add up to be investing over paying it off quickly. As the experts in chapter 5 mention, it's usually a good strategy to save for retirement first and then focus additional funds on paying off student loans carrying interest rates above 5 percent.

2. It felt like a symbolic gesture of us coming together as a financial team. It would no longer be "your money" and "my money" or "your student loans," but rather "our money" and "our student loans."

There was just one snafu. I didn't know how to even go about cashing out of my mutual fund, and I needed to learn more about the tax implications of such a move. Did it really make sense to sell and pay taxes on the capital gains in order to put it toward debt?

THIS CHAPTER DEALS specifically with selling an investment in a taxable account—not a tax-deferred account like an IRA or 401(k). If you take money out of a retirement account and you're under fifty-nine and a half, it could be subject to ordinary taxes in addition to a penalty for early withdrawal. That's a whole lot worse than what you'd pay on regular taxable investments.

WHEN TO SELL AN INVESTMENT

Ah, if only I had a really prescriptive answer to that question! There is a variety of reasons you might elect to sell an investment. It could be as simple as tax-loss harvesting or rebalancing your portfolio. Maybe your investment is like my mutual fund example: the time horizon has come to its natural conclusion and you're ready to use the investment for its intended purpose. Or perhaps your risk tolerance has changed and you want to be more or less aggressive and need to off-load the investment to achieve that purpose. Or maybe it's just a dud and you've given it time to perform and are ready to cut it loose.

HOW TO SELL AN INVESTMENT

This depends on what the investment is and how you're investing. Maybe you have an advisor or broker you can call up and ask to make the sale for you. But if you're a DIY investor or use a robo-advisor or app, then you generally just log in and request to make a sale or withdrawal. Just be sure you list it as a "market sell order" and don't accidentally end up buying more!

You could "dollar-cost-average" your way out of the market, which means you don't take it all out in one lump sum. Instead, you take portions out over the span of weeks, months, or even years. You'd do this in order to hedge your bets on the value going up while you start moving the money to a more conservative investment (or cash). That way, as you continue to divest, you're selling it at higher and higher prices. Obviously, this can backfire and you could dollar-cost-average out and hit the market at lower points.

DO YOU NEED TO BUY NEW INVESTMENTS TO KEEP YOUR PORTFOLIO DIVERSIFIED?

Rebalancing your portfolio is one reason to sell an investment. Let's look at the example of me selling my mutual fund. In that case, the mutual fund was moderately aggressive and invested in large-cap growth funds. By selling the fund, I didn't put my overall portfolio out of whack because I had other index funds that were moderately aggressive to aggressive and invested in similar large-cap companies.

But let's look at an overly simplistic example for the sake of demonstrating when you may need to buy a new investment:

You own stock in large-cap companies covering five different sectors: energy, technology, health care, real estate, and consumer staples. You decide to sell your technology-sector stock. Now your portfolio is missing investment in a major sector of the stock market, so it would be prudent to replace that investment with a different tech stock.

Remember, diversification is about more than stocks versus bonds versus cash equivalents. It's also about owning in different sectors of the market.

THE TAX IMPLICATIONS OF SELLING OR MAKING A WITHDRAWAL

Sorry to say, but selling investments for a profit means Uncle Sam is going to come calling. You've made income, and now the IRS wants its cut. You can be taxed on dividends, capital gains, or interest income. You don't have to pay taxes at the moment of the sale or withdrawal. That bill will come at tax time, when your brokerage sends you a 1099-B form and/or a 1099-DIV. It's important that you have a rough estimate of how much you'll owe on your taxes, so you have that money set aside and earmarked for tax season. This is especially critical if you're used to getting a refund and therefore don't normally have a stash of cash to pay what you owe in taxes. That could be a most unpleasant surprise.

In a point on the scoreboard for online financial advisors (aka robo-advisors): Investing via a robo-advisor generally means it does some of the heavy lifting when it comes to minimizing taxes. Betterment, for instance, offers a Tax Impact Preview, so you can see approximately how much your potential move will cost you.

The amount you'll owe in taxes depends on your tax bracket, how much you earned on the sale, the type of investment it was, and when you sold the investment relative to its purchase date.

When Did You Buy the Investment?

The sale of an investment that's less than a year old could mean you owe short-term capital gains tax.

Capital Gains

Capital gains are the profit you made on your investment, assuming you sold it for a profit. The tax rate for long-term capital gains is usually 15 to 20 percent, depending on your tax bracket.* Short-term capital gains are taxed at the same rate as ordinary income, from 10 percent all the way up to 37 percent.

Dividends

Your mutual fund, index fund, ETF, or stock may pay you dividends for being a shareholder. You can take these dividends as income and pay taxes on them, or you can reinvest them to purchase more shares. Dividends can be "qualified" or "nonqualified." Dividends are qualified if you hold the investment for sixty days or more and if they are a payment from the common stock of a US corporation. Qualified dividends are taxed like capital gains, at 0, 15, and 20 percent, depending on your tax bracket, while nonqualified dividends are taxed at your ordinary income tax bracket. Tax law is subject to change, so you should always check IRS .gov for recent information about current tax law with regard to capital gains and dividends.

Interest Income

This is just like how you owe money earned on interest sitting in your savings account. Any interest earned on bonds, CDs, money market products, or similar cash equivalents is subject to tax. This interest will be reported on either a 1099-DIV or a 1099-INT form.

Can You Deduct a Loss?

If your losses outweighed your gains, then you may be able to write them off on your taxes. Moments like this are when it can pay to hire someone who knows all the ins and outs of tax code in relation to investing.

---

*It depends on your tax bracket specific to long-term capital gains and dividends, not your ordinary income tax bracket. These changes occurred under the Tax Cuts and Jobs Act.

Foreign Stock

Having foreign stock in your portfolio, which most well-diversified portfolios do, could also mean you owe foreign taxes on any dividends earned. Oftentimes your brokerage will handle this for mutual funds and ETFs and the taxes owed will be taken out of your dividends.

WILL YOU OWE ANY FEES?

There may be more than tax implications attached to selling an investment. Don't forget to review your brokerage's fees. With "trade fees" on your stocks and back-end-load mutual funds, you'll need to sell enough and have a strong enough profit to cover not just the taxes you'll owe but also the fee your brokerage will charge when you sell.

CHECKLIST FOR SELLING YOUR INVESTMENTS

❏ Have you given your investment enough time to perform, or are you getting trigger happy and contemplating selling after a few months?

❏ Do the math and determine approximately how much you may owe in capital gains tax, then put that money aside for your tax bill. (Be aware that selling in less than a year means paying more in taxes due to short-term capital gains.)

❏ How much are the fees you'll need to pay (if any)?

❏ Should you replace this investment with something else to stay diversified?

Chapter 14

Tactics the Wealthy Use to Make and Preserve Money

ONE OF THE GOALS I (half-jokingly) set for myself in my early twenties was to beat my dad to being a millionaire. Except, without context, that sounds pretty cruel. It's not that I, at thirty-two years his junior, wanted to have a million dollars in the bank before he did. (That game is long over.) It's that I wanted to do it earlier in life than he had.

WATCHING A SELF-MADE MILLIONAIRE HAPPEN

My dad set a goal at twenty-four to be a millionaire by the time he reached forty-two. He didn't have the advantage of being gifted family money starting out or even having the cost of his college education or MBA covered by his parents. He started investing early and saving aggressively. In fact, he took out a loan when he started his MBA program just so he could invest the money. He sold the investment when he graduated to pay back the loan and pocketed the difference. Then he learned how to make himself a highly valuable employee.

As a child, I observed two things about my dad: he loved running, and he was always listening to language cassette tapes. Around the time I turned seven or eight, he started traveling to Japan for work—so he decided to learn Japanese. I don't know all the details of how and why we ended up moving to Japan when I was ten, but I imagine my dad's dedication to learning both Japanese customs and the language certainly helped him be the one picked for the expat assignment.

Once we got sent overseas, my parents lived so below their means that they were able to save about 80 percent of my dad's income. Not that my sister, Cailin, or I knew any different. My parents didn't upgrade our lifestyle. In fact, my mom's Nike gym shorts from the 1990s were a source of real tension in my teen years. I remember trying to throw them out once or twice. My parents didn't buy flashy jewelry or home furnishings or tech toys. The only time they really seemed to splurge was when we traveled.

These lessons in frugality and self-reliance were passed down not only through example, but because my parents weren't big on handing us money. Cailin and I were encouraged to be entrepreneurial if we wanted money to make a purchase. We were big on the babysitting circuit, and also created a mini pet-sitting empire one summer. We also dabbled in modeling and acting overseas. Some pachinko game in Japan may still have my voice-over congratulating people on their win.

On the occasions my parents would help subsidize a purchase, it would be up to 50 percent. This family rule extended all the way through to our college educations. If Cailin and I wanted to graduate debt free, then we'd need to earn scholarships in order to subsidize 50 percent of our educations. (Spoiler: we both did. After a fraught decision-making process, I realized it made more sense to go to a smaller, lesser-known school that was offering me academic scholarships and come out debt free than to go to a popular, name-brand school and graduate with $80,000 in debt.)

Then, my parents moved back to America after an eleven-year stint living overseas. Within two years, my dad, a longtime company man, got fired. He could've called it quits then and retired early, in his mid-fifties. My parents had a comfortable but not lavish lifestyle that could've been supported by their investment portfolio at that point. However, my parents decided to keep working. My mom became a real estate agent, and my dad created his own consulting company.

At first, their goals were to avoid digging into their nest egg and to make enough income to replace what my dad had been earning when he worked for a company. He didn't think it would be possible, but in less than half a year, it became apparent that he could not only replace his former salary, but earn significantly more. He's now earning more as a consultant than he did at the peak of his career working for a company.

My dad credits two big things for this lucrative career pivot. The first is technology. It's a much different world than when he started his career in the 1980s, and technology enables us to make and foster relationships in a whole new way. The second is his marriage to my mom. They've always been a team, and she's such a strong support system. She didn't shut down the idea of uprooting the family and moving to Asia or panic when my dad got fired after they repatriated back to the United States.

I give you all this context to provide some insight into how my parents' minds worked. These are people who built a multimillion-dollar portfolio by the time they were in their fifties without the advantage of an inheritance. Of course, you could point to the fact that both are white, able-bodied, straight Americans. There is privilege in all those factors. But that doesn't discount the fact that they achieved a great financial feat.

I'm incredibly fortunate both to have grown up with a blueprint for how to become a millionaire and to have received the benefits that a financially stable home affords. While I didn't know my parents' net worth until years after I graduated college, I knew we never struggled to cover basic needs, and my parents didn't fight about money while I was growing up.

It's also no coincidence that my sister and I are both self-employed and entrepreneurial in our careers. We were encouraged by our parents to figure out how to creatively meet our financial desires as children, but we also, consciously or not, know we have the Bank of Mom and Dad for a bailout.

I've never filled out a loan application at the Bank of Mom and Dad, but a friend once asked me, "Do you really think you'd take as much career risk if your parents couldn't help you out?" Being the risk-averse person I am, he raised a sage point. I probably wouldn't have been willing to take as much risk without knowing I could receive help if everything went wrong in my life tomorrow.

But I've digressed from the original point. I want to beat my dad to a million dollars. Sure, some of that's rooted in my innately competitive nature. But more of it stems from knowing that achieving double-comma net worth, especially without an inheritance, would make my dad incredibly proud.

Except, becoming a millionaire by forty-two wouldn't actually be beating him. You have to adjust for inflation. I'd need about $1.5 million by age forty-two in order for it to be the same achievement. So, my goal is to hit a million-dollar net worth by thirty-five years old.

Despite the fact that I've seen how this could be achieved in my own home, I'm still a bit obsessive with every self-made millionaire story the media puts out. We all love a good "How I Became a Millionaire" tale, especially if it feels like something we can decode and reverse-engineer for our own gain. It's why those listicle articles with headlines like "The 10 Books Every Millionaire Reads" or "5 Easy Steps This Self-Made Millionaire Took to Get Rich" or "7 Mistakes to Avoid If You Want to Retire in Your 30s" remain incredibly popular.

After speaking with so many women and men who have spent their careers in the financial services and wealth management industries, I just had to ask, "What are the wealthy doing differently that the average Millennial should know?" Here's what they had to say.

ASHLEY FOX, FINANCIAL EDUCATION SPECIALIST AND FOUNDER OF EMPIFY

Fox started her career in asset management for JPMorgan Chase, where she worked with high-net-worth individuals whose assets exceeded $25 million. She left her job to build her own business and now works to empower others to build financial success.

Wealthy people value legacy. Everything they do is not for today. For instance, people say, "I want to buy stocks. I want to make money real quick." Everything is temporary, whereas wealthy people think of longevity. How can my kids' kids' kids never have to financially struggle? How can my kids' kids' kids run this business I've created?

I think we get so consumed with getting rich quick for a temporary fix, and I think that *wealth* is generational; *rich* is having a lot of money right now. Wealthy people focus on the preservation of assets and the protection of their assets. Wealthy people don't operate from a survival perspective, even if they didn't have money, their mind-sets are totally different. What they value, where they travel, what they read, what they do with their time, whom they associate themselves with, it's all for the betterment of making them stronger people. They're not just trying to figure out "How can I make this money real quick so I can buy this?" It's "How can I grow this business and protect my assets, put it in a trust fund for my kids, so my kids will be set for college?"

If you take private equity, for instance, they're setting aside money for five or ten years. They're not worried about today; they're focused on tomorrow. The average person only cares about today, and they're trying to survive today.

Fox then shared some of her memories of working with high-net-worth individuals and the eye-opening moments she experienced:

I sat in rooms with clients who bought art for a living. They had nice, fancy clothes and they bought art.* Buying art helped to build

---

*This is actually a really fascinating example of how the wealthy think differently. I highly recommend checking out NPR's *Planet Money* episode 823: "Planet Monet," which digs into the world of buying, selling, and storing art as a means of protecting your wealth and shielding yourself from paying taxes.

and protect their wealth. The transferring of art from country to country is one way you can preserve money and minimize taxes. For me, it made me think "What the hell are you doing sitting behind a desk when there are people who buy art for a living and you're sitting here running their portfolios and creating their presentations so that they can keep their money?"

I would see trust-fund babies where the parents would build everything for them and we would sit in meetings and tell them how they were blowing through their money, and eventually it would go to zero. Which made me realize it's not about the amount of money; it's the mind-set the person has around money.

Now, this might be a little technical. We had a client who built a company years ago. There's something called a GRAT [or grantor-retained annuity trust, which is used to transfer wealth and typically enables the recipient to avoid paying gift or estate taxes]. You can put an appreciable asset into a GRAT, and it'll pay you distributions every quarter or every year or every month until the GRAT's time limit is up.

What I saw happen was a guy who built a company—and I use the product he created to this day—[had] his company [get] bought by a large Fortune 500 company while his asset was inside the GRAT. That would be like founding Instagram and putting part of Instagram's ownership into a GRAT. In the midst of that, Instagram gets bought by Facebook, so now your company went from being worth $500,000 to $1 billion. If you took that money out of the GRAT, you would've made some money and had to pay capital gains tax. But because it was inside the GRAT, and you give that portion to your heirs, you don't have to pay taxes. I watched someone save $60 million in taxes. He'd gotten to the point where he had too much money and didn't need anymore, so all he cared about was protecting it and not paying taxes.

What made it more real is that I use the original company's products and the products of the company that bought his company. Working with him made everything so real and possible, but I realized I was on the wrong end of the table. Why am I keeping him rich? Who is making Ashley rich? I was trained to see what real money was, and it made me feel that the game I was playing was too small. Then I realized I wasn't even playing the game—I was on the sidelines making sure the players were fit to play. But no, I deserve to be in this game, too.

SALLIE KRAWCHECK, COFOUNDER AND CEO OF ELLEVEST

Krawcheck has been in wealth management for more than twenty years. She served as the CEO of Merrill Lynch Wealth Management and of Smith Barney before cofounding Ellevest.

I know very few people who inherited money. The people I know oftentimes got into the right business line at the right time and worked their tails off. For some, it was in financial services in a period of time before that took off. For some, it was in technology as that took off. For some, they went to China. This is advice we don't often give young people. It is so much easier for you to be successful and for your wealth to grow if you're in a company or business that is growing or if you're in a country that is growing.

If you're in a company that grows 10 percent a year and you are average, you're growing at 10 percent a year. If, on the other hand, you're at a company that's shrinking 10 percent a year, you have to be 10 percent better than everybody else in order to stay still. Then to really grow, you have to be 20 or 30 percent better than everybody else—and nobody is.

When you think of something like traditional media, there aren't a lot of people that are thirty-five years old and went into traditional media right out of college who are very wealthy right now. Maybe there are a few, but those are exceptional individuals.

However, there are a lot of people who went to Wall Street in their early twenties who did very well with technology. It sounds so obvious, but I don't know that we really emphasize that it's important to pick the right company, the right industry. It's easy to say and, of course, much harder to do. Make sure you're always thinking about industry dynamic before you join an industry and company dynamic before you join a company.

COLLEEN JACONETTI, CPA, CFP®

Jaconetti is a senior investment analyst at Vanguard Investment Strategy Group, with more than fifteen years of experience in the financial services industry.

Save early and often. People don't amass a ton of wealth without saving. Being knowledgeable about what you're investing in and the cost of what you're investing in makes a big difference. I wouldn't say from an investment perspective that people who are very wealthy do anything differently. They still need to broadly diversify. They still don't want to overpay for the quality of products they're receiving. They're just in a different spot as far as they may or may not have debt. Some still may have debt if they're buying multiple properties and balancing debt and savings.

The financial decisions of how to invest may not be dramatically different, unless people are going outside the stock market and investing in their summer home with the idea of renting it out when they're retired. Or they could be using gifting strategies because they have so much money they're managing taxes. That's not an investing conversation as much as a tax and financial planning conversation.

When it comes to investing, everyone has the same principals of rebalancing, diversifying, and buying assets in the right spot, but are they more aggressive? Are they overweighting certain factors in the market or certain sectors? They may be doing that because they can afford to lose that amount of money, whereas other people may not be as comfortable. It comes back to the fact that they may have a higher risk tolerance than people who don't have as much wealth yet. Although, sometimes when you've amassed a lot of wealth, it's actually the opposite. Why should I take risk? If I have $5 million saved, I'm comfortable. I've had client conversations where they're comfortable in 100 percent bonds because they don't need any more money, and instead of shooting for the stars, they'd rather pass on money to a charity or to family members rather than taking a risk of the $5 million dropping to $3 million.

BRANDON KRIEG, CEO AND COFOUNDER OF STASH

Krieg spent fifteen years working as a trader on Wall Street before leaving to launch Stash, a micro-investing app.

That's me, I'm completely self-made. I do not come from money. I think I had about three hundred bucks on me when I moved to New York onto my friend's couch. I can tell you, forgetting about myself, just seeing what my friends are doing—and I have a lot of friends who are owners of hedge funds and very successful—they do exactly what Stash does. They are very well diversified in their investments, and they continue to add to their investments on a regular basis. So, when they get more cash, they buy more of their investments. I've been seeing that for a long time. That's how I've been seeing the best investors treat their own money.

It's funny, I look at my really successful friends, and no one trades. The thing about money in general and gaining wealth is that there is no fast money. I don't believe in fast money. I don't think fast money is real. Fast money leaves you just as fast as it comes to you. There aren't get-rich-quick schemes in investing. Most get-rich-quick schemes, they're Ponzi schemes, or illegal.

For me it's time-tested things that work, for both the super-successful and wealthy as well as beginners. Be well diversified and keep adding money all the time.

JILL SCHLESINGER, CFP®, CBS NEWS BUSINESS ANALYST AND AUTHOR OF *THE DUMB THINGS SMART PEOPLE DO WITH THEIR MONEY*

Schlesinger started her career as an options trader, then spent fourteen years working for an independent investment advisory firm before becoming the host of the *BetterOff* podcast and the nationally syndicated radio show *Jill on Money*.

The dirty little secret is that it's not complicated. They just either inherit wealth and don't squander it and live within their means, or if they don't have access to money, they just start saving early. Guests on my podcast start by answering, "What's the best financial decision you ever made?" Forty percent of those answers from successful people are "I started saving early." "I opened an IRA in 1986 with $2,000, and I just kept doing it every year." It doesn't matter as much how well you do, your performance. It matters that you save, and no one in the industry wants to actually say that, but that's really the simple truth.

DOUGLAS A. BONEPARTH, CFP®, FOUNDER OF BONE FIDE WEALTH

New York City's financial advisor for Millennials, Boneparth spent eight years working as a financial advisor before attending NYU's Stern School of Business and then launching his own financial advisor practice.

Patience. Many of these people did not build their wealth over-
night. The amount of time, energy, and money—meaning their
own investment in themselves and in their businesses—should be
the focus. Getting caught up in the allure of the fact that they actually are wealthy is not the lesson at hand. Ask yourself, "What
did this person do to reach that level of success or accomplish-
ment?" Figure out how you can replicate that in the context of
your own financial life. Every time someone goes by in a nice
Porsche, I used to think, "Oh, that guy's lucky." Now I think, "They
worked their ass off." Or "All flash and no cash." You never know
who is leasing that Bentley and who bought it in cash!

MARIA BRUNO, CFP®, SENIOR INVESTMENT ANALYST
AT VANGUARD INVESTMENT STRATEGY GROUP

Bruno is part of the team responsible for establishing and overseeing the
investment philosophy, methodology, and portfolio construction strategies supporting Vanguard's advisory services, products, and strategies.
She's worked in the financial services industry for more than twenty
years.

So, the one thing that comes into my mind would be income taxes.
So, the wealthy are high-income earners, and they may be more
engaged in how to think about taxes and how income taxes or
even estate taxes come into play in their decision making.

   With Millennials or young investors, really, the key is to save
and, really, it's resource allocation. And the wealthy may not have
that decision making because they, fortunately, may not have con-
straints in terms of resource allocation. But for young investors,
it's really about how do I decide in terms of how to maximize my
savings while also paying down debt? It's that balancing act.

JENNIFER BARRETT, CHIEF EDUCATION OFFICER FOR ACORNS

Barrett is an award-winning financial journalist with more than fifteen years' experience. Before Acorns, she worked for CNBC and DailyWorth.

I think they just build wealth. That is part of the strategy from the get-go. It's this idea of "getting by" versus "building wealth." It's not just in the mind-set, but there is a lot of it inherent in the mind-set. If you feel like you're getting by paycheck to paycheck, it's a struggle, then you're not building toward something. You're stuck in one place treading water. For the wealthy, from the beginning, the idea is "How do I take what I have and build more from that? How do I put this money to work for me?"

It's interesting because I've been in this space for so long, and I read Tony Robbins's money book, and there was one part that resonated so strongly with me. The way he talks about doing this calculation: "What is the point at which your basic expenses will be covered from the returns you're making on your investments? And what would you be willing to live on at that point?" So, it is kind of a retirement question, but for me, I didn't know what my number is. I'm just putting money aside. I think everyone is kind of like that, and thinking, "I'm just going to sock a lot of money away, and I hope I get this right and don't outlive my frickin' money."

So, I started working on it, and I thought, "What are the minimum expenses we have and what would I need to get to so that I could hypothetically quit my job and just do whatever it is I want to do and be okay?" And that was a real number. Now, for the first time, I have a real number and an idea in my head of what age that could be and what it would take to hit that number at earlier ages. That's a very different way of looking at how you're building your wealth.

It doesn't have to be that specifically, but that's what clicked for me. I don't want to wait until I'm sixty-five or seventy to retire. I want to be slowly moving toward a place where I have more flexibility and can do a wide range of things that interest me, and I don't want that to be on hold until I'm sixty-five or seventy. So how do I make that happen? By constantly looking at how you can continue to build on your wealth. And you don't have to start wealthy to get into that mind-set. You have to stop thinking about your situation as being paycheck-to-paycheck survival mode and really sit down and figure out how can you start getting ahead today.

A CHECKLIST FOR WHAT THE WEALTHY ARE DOING

I know, I know, those are a lot of long stories, and we're Millennials who are used to reading tweet-size descriptions of things. So, here's a checklist of what the wealthy are doing (not necessarily all that differently).

❑ The wealthy think in terms of longevity instead of temporary survival, even before they were wealthy and were in survival mode. They focus on building companies and assets that will last for generations.

❑ It's a mind-set shift. Even if they didn't come from money, their mind-set is always about how to better themselves and their situation, all the way down to what they read, how they spend their time, and with whom they associate.

❑ They save early and consistently.

❑ They're strategic about careers by picking companies, industries, and even countries with growth potential.

❑ They're patient.

❏ They consider how to minimize the impact of taxes on their income, investments, and legacy.

❏ They have a number in mind for financial independence (when they can live off the returns on their investments) that's not a guesstimate.

Chapter 15

Where Can I Get More Investing Advice (Because I've Been on Reddit . . .)?

ANY QUESTION WE HAVE these days can usually be answered in seconds. That's a low-risk proposition when you're in a debate with a friend at the bar or if you're trying to find out which restaurants are still serving at 2:00 a.m. It's a high-risk proposition when it comes to your money. Finding the correct, credible, helpful, easy-to-understand answer isn't always as simple as typing your question into a search bar and hitting Enter. Figuring out where to learn more about investing can feel just as overwhelming as actually understanding the stock market. There are so many gurus, coaches, and self-proclaimed experts making big promises about your results that it's easy to get hoodwinked.

One thing to consider is that anyone offering a free service ultimately needs to get paid. It's rare that people provide value without anything in return. That "in return" could be as simple as collecting your email address for a mailing list that can later be used to try to convert you into a paying client. I'm not condemning this. I don't think people should give away all their services for free. I'm simply pointing out that free courses and services are rarely truly "free."

Here is a long list of options for you to consider, broken down by type of resource.

HIGHLY TECHNICAL SITES

These sites may be a bit heavy-handed when it comes to the technical jargon, but they're completely worth a visit.

- *FINRA.org:* Visit this site, or just go directly to FINRA.org/investors to find articles, tools, and calculators. There is even a section dedicated to general financial well-being, like building your emergency fund and paying off debt.
- *Investopedia.com:* I hesitate to put this under "Highly Technical" because I worry you'll think it's inaccessible. It's not. Investopedia is a treasure trove of information about pretty much any investing-related question you could think up. While there is some jargon, the text is written in a way that's meant to be easily digestible. It's hard to write about investing without bringing in the jargon (trust me, I know at this point!).
- *Investor.gov:* This is the SEC's educational website, and probably more applicable than SEC.gov itself. Its compound interest calculator is one of my favorite online tools. The website introduces investing and how to research and protect your investments.
- *Morningstar:* Morningstar has all the market news, plus it analyzes and rates mutual funds and ETFs on a one-to-five-star scale. That's a gold mine for rookie investors who need some reassurance (and even for seasoned investors).
- *SEC.gov:* Perfect if you really want to nerd out over the regulatory side of investing.
- *SIFMA.org:* The Securities Industry and Financial Markets Association (SIFMA) is really geared toward industry professionals. Similar to SEC.gov, it's for anyone looking to do a deep dive into investing industry issues. The really technical side of things, like

"international trade and investment," "capital formation," and "equity market structure."

MEDIA OUTLETS

There is a wealth of information at your fingertips thanks to the internet. Granted, some of these outlets live behind a paywall . . . but here is a variety of top media outlets for investing and financial news.

- Bloomberg
- CNBC
- CNNMoney
- *Financial Times*
- Kiplinger
- MarketWatch
- The Motley Fool (fool.com)
- *The New York Times*
  - *DealBook* is the *New York Times* business and policy newsletter
- Reuters
- TheStreet
- *The Wall Street Journal*
- Yahoo! Finance

PODCASTS

Podcasts are one of my favorite ways to consume media. You can learn something new while walking the dog, going to work, on a flight—you get it. Here are some of the great podcasts out there to help you shore up your investing or just general money knowledge.

- *Afford Anything:* Paula Pant covers all sorts of topics on her podcast *Afford Anything,* which focuses on the notion that you can afford anything, just not everything. She switches it up between long-form interviews with guests and Q&As from her listeners. Paula herself is something of a real estate mogul, so her home ownership episodes are always worth a listen if you're interested in getting into the real estate investing game.

- *Better Off*: Jill Schlesinger's podcast digs into all kinds of money questions. She provides short episodes in which she answers questions and longer-form episodes with guest interviews.

- *The Investors Podcast*: You want hard-core investing information? This podcast offers insights from billionaires and other high-net-worth individuals. Their tagline is "We Study Billionaires," so you know it'll have some interesting investing insights.

- *Marketplace* and *Marketplace Morning Report*: Both podcasts bring you the latest in financial news, the markets, and business world.

- *Planet Money*: It's not specifically an investing podcast, but *Planet Money* is one of my all-time favorite money podcasts. It does a great job of doing interesting deep dives (not always easy) into different money-related issues.

- *Unchained:* For those interested in cryptocurrency (which I know some of you certainly are), *Unchained* by Laura Shin can deepen your knowledge of the cryptocurrency Blockchain to a point where you can be an educated investor.

BOOKS

The book you've just read is a primer on investing. There is plenty more to learn! Here are some books to check out as you continue on your journey.

The Classics

- *The Intelligent Investor*, Benjamin Graham: Benjamin Graham is often cited as the father of value investing. He taught Warren Buffett, who practices value investing himself. Even though Graham's book was first published in 1949, it lives on (and has been updated along the way) as a defining text on investing.
- *The Little Book of Common Sense Investing*, John C. Bogle: Bogle is the godfather of index funds and the founder of Vanguard. Naturally, this book focuses on the strategy behind index fund investing and why investing really comes down to common sense.
- *A Random Walk Down Wall Street*, Burton G. Malkiel: This is one of the most recommended investing books out there. It's a hefty book with *a lot* of information but an excellent pick if you're looking to level up even more.

Still Finding Your Footing

- *The Pocket Idiot's Guide to Investing in Stocks:* This is one of the first investing books I read. It's focused specifically on stocks, and while there's a lot more to investing than just understanding stocks, it's a simple overview and worth a read.
- *The Simple Path to Wealth*, J. L. Collins: Collins's book hasn't been around for decades like some of the classics, but it's destined to be a classic in its own right. Inspired by letters to his daughter, Collins wrote the book to help people navigate investing. It's also peppered with some other financial advice and gives some direct recommendations about products and brokerages.
- *Stock Market Investing: Mini-Lessons for Beginners: A Starter Guide for Beginner Investors*, Mabel Nuñez: Nuñez really digs into all the mechanics behind investing in the stock market in this guide, which is a natural extension of this high-level overview you've just finished reading.

Interesting Reading

- *The Ascent of Money,* Niall Ferguson: If you're a history nerd, and especially if you enjoyed chapter 11, then you're this book's target audience. Ferguson takes readers on a journey through the creation of our modern financial system. I swear, it's more interesting than it may sound to you right now.
- *The Thin Green Line,* Paul Sullivan: This is an entire book dedicated to the question "What are the wealthy doing differently than you?" Sullivan, a *New York Times* reporter, pulls back the curtain and shows the financial behaviors of America's wealthy.

RESOURCES FROM BROKERAGE FIRMS, ROBO-ADVISORS, AND APPS

Many brokerage firms, investment banks, and financial apps offer education portals or blogs. Obviously, all these resources are given with the hopes of converting you into a client, but they're still free and available for you to use. Here are some of the places you can find tools, calculators, checklists, and articles.

- *Acorns:* Acorns offers a website specifically geared toward financial education called Grow from Acorns (https://grow.acorns.com). You don't need to be a customer to gain access; you can get the basics in its "Money 101" section, read more about financial news, and find how-to guides and interviews with financial gurus and even celebrities.
- *Fidelity:* Fidelity.com offers a "Planning and Advice" section that's available to non-clients. You can find budget calculators and tips, recommendations for how to build and protect your wealth, checklists for what to do after certain life stages (e.g., marriage), and more.
- *Vanguard:* Vanguard.com's personal investor portal is filled with calculators, worksheets, and tools for both clients and non-clients.

You can answer some questions to determine your ideal asset allocation, compare investments, estimate the income you'd need in retirement, and set goals for the future.

- *Betterment:* Betterment's "Retirement Planning" center does a great job of being Millennial focused. There's even an IRA calculator to help you answer the question "Roth or Traditional: which is better?" You can also find general personal finance advice as well as investing 101 and advanced investing.
- *Charles Schwab:* Schwab.com's "Retirement & Planning" section is filled with guides to help get you from where you are today to a comfortable retirement. It even includes advice on insurance basics, taxes, estate planning, and what to do during life events such as job loss, marriage, divorce, and having children.
- *Stash:* StashLearn is a big part of the Stash website, which you can access without being a customer. Articles range from topics like "If cannabis is illegal under federal law, how is it legal to invest in it?" to "What is a portfolio?" to "What's a trade gap and what can it mean for the economy?"
- *T. Rowe Price:* The website's "Planning & Research" section helps you along your journey. There is an "Investing 101" guide (but you do have this book for that), as well as calculators, research, analysis, and insights.
- *WealthFront:* Robo-advisor WealthFront provides clients and non-clients access to the company's blog. The blog tends to be on the more technical side, with articles such as "Investing Insights," "Planning & Taxes," "Retirement," and "Stock Options & RSUs."
- *Wealthsimple: Wealthsimple Magazine,* the company's online blog, is available to anyone. It spans from technical stories to how-to guides to the more emotional accounts in its "Money Diaries" series.

ONLINE RESOURCES

The internet is a magical land, but it's also the Wild, Wild West of un-checked and unregulated financial advice. You can find some quality, actionable advice, but you can also be led disastrously astray if you're not careful. You should always bear in mind that the writer doesn't know you, your time horizon, your goals, or your risk tolerance when he or she dishes out advice geared for the masses. Just because a portfolio strategy is working for one blogger who claims to be a millionaire doesn't mean it'll work for you. Take all advice with a dash of salt and proceed with ample caution.

Now that I've issued a big warning, here are some places you can go to learn more.

Personal Finance Blogs

- *Building Bread:* Kevin L. Matthews II is a licensed financial advisor who is hell-bent on ensuring you know how to build generational wealth. His website is full of useful resources and guides, and his Facebook Live videos are hilarious and engaging.
- *The Dumpster Dog Blog:* It's as irreverent as it sounds. Amanda Holden, aka the Dumpster Dog, worked in the investment industry in San Francisco for six years. Now she's helping young women focus on investing through her writing, talks, and business "Invested Development." She's a deep thinker who writes about more than just investing, and there 100 percent should be a parental advisory label on many of her posts. She's a great fit if you like quirky humor.
- *Financial Samurai:* Sam Dogen is a former Wall Street guy who spent thirteen years in the financial services world, including time at Goldman Sachs. He is incredibly analytical and shares insights on everything from how to better engineer your career to building a healthy net worth.
- *Girl$ on the Money:* Mabel Nuñez is a self-proclaimed "first gener-

ation investor" because no one in her family or immediate circle of friends had ever invested before. She became fascinated by investing in college and started investing herself right as the market was crashing in 2008. She is passionate about helping others, especially women, learn about and feel confident investing.

- *Jlcollinsnh.com/stock-series:* J. L. Collins, the author of the aforementioned *The Simple Path to Wealth*, started it all on his blog. His "Stock Series" is one of the most highly regarded among money blogger nerds.
- *Nerd's Eye View:* A self-described financial planning nerd, Michael Kitces writes for advisors, but there's a lot you can learn from him. Some writing may feel a bit high level when you're starting out, but just give it a chance.
- *Oblivious Investor:* Mike Piper is a CPA who does an excellent job of presenting the pros and cons when evaluating investing strategies. His insights about how to minimize your taxes as an investor are incredibly valuable.
- *Tela Holcomb:* Interested in getting into some of the nitty-gritty of individual stock picking? Holcomb reviews her strategies and digs into her monthly returns in videos on her website, TelaHolcomb.com.

Reddit

I love lurking on Reddit's money-related threads sometimes because there is a gem of an insight and other times because it's interesting to watch people get into such intense conversations over money. But mostly I enjoy it because it's fodder for potential articles. There are story ideas aplenty on Reddit.

"If you're on an investing thread on Reddit, the advice you're getting there is worth exactly what you paid for it," says Sallie Krawcheck, CEO of Ellevest. Krawcheck is right. Reddit can be interesting, but be wary of free, crowdsourced advice you find on blogs and online platforms. Always check it against other credible sources.

COURSES

There are plenty of online and in-person courses out there in the world, but always be really discerning. Consider how a course is marketed. Remember that if it seems too good to be true, then it probably is. People should not be promising you specific returns on your investments after you've completed a course. If the course is free, then oftentimes there's going to be a bid for an upsell at some point—content creators need to get paid.

You can always search for investing courses at your local community college or by using online platforms like Coursera, Udemy, or Khan Academy.

FIND THE THING THAT SUITS YOU BEST

We all learn in different ways. Just because your best friend swears by a certain book or gushes about a particular podcast doesn't mean it'll be what speaks to you. Don't be discouraged if it takes some searching to find the right fit, but it's out there. There's a Cinderella and a glass slipper reference here just waiting to be made!

Conclusion

Now It's Time to Level Up!

WELL, HELLO AGAIN!

Congrats on finishing this book (or skipping to the end). You've now got the tools and hopefully the gumption to go out and start investing. Well, as long as you've got your financial oxygen mask firmly affixed to your face, you're allowed to start investing.

While I was doing research for this book and interviewing experts, Jill Schlesinger's words stuck with me most: "Know that if you can't do it, it's not the worst thing in the world, it's just that you've got to save a lot more money. Your money, when you invest it, is doing some of the lifting for you. When you're completely risk averse, it just means you're going to have to save a lot more money to reach your goals."

It's strange to end an entire book about investing by saying, "Hey, you don't have to invest if you don't want to." But I respect the way Schlesinger positioned that sentiment.

There is a risk to investing, and there's definitely work to do in order to start and continue investing. You must do your research. You need to rebalance and modify investments as your goals change. There's no "set it and forget it" here. Being an investor means being proactive and really taking control of your financial future. It's what I want for you. It's what I wish for everyone.

But I'm reasonable. I understand that some people, no matter how much you explain the mechanics behind and importance of investing, are going to resist the idea. Taking even the smallest amount of risk is nauseating to them. So, in Schlesinger's words, "it just means you're going to have to save a lot more money to reach your goals." Just keep that in mind if this book hasn't put your anxiety at ease.

Investing is, in some regard, a wealth equalizer. Are you going to become a multibillionaire-level wealthy person just through tried-and-true saving and investing techniques? Meh, probably not, but you can achieve financial independence and at least a million, if not several million, dollars in your lifetime if you start young (or now), set goals, rebalance in accordance with how your life and goals change, and, perhaps most important, stay consistent.

Don't let another day, week, month, or year go by with you thinking that you can't invest because it's too complicated or you aren't rich enough or whatever other excuse you might've allowed to creep into your brain thus far. In fact, set down one investing goal right here for what you want to achieve within one year of today's date. Go on, write it down.

One year from today, ___/ ___/ _____, my goal is to:

_____

_____

_____

_____

_____

Now look at that goal and see what small step you can take each month to make it happen. Break it down into small, achievable, consistent actions.

You can take control. It's time for you to Level Up Your Money! #LUYM.

Share your investing journey experiences, thoughts, and questions with me and others on Twitter and Instagram using #LUYM and tagging @BrokeMillennial on Twitter and @BrokeMillennialBlog on Instagram.

Best of luck,
Erin

Acknowledgments

To my dad, who provided much of my foundational knowledge of investing, allowed me to write about his journey, and always was at the other end of the line when I need guidance in my financial (and regular) life.

This book was written and edited while I was also planning my wedding, so a huge thank-you goes to my mom, who stepped in and took over so much of the wedding planning in order to allow me to focus on my career. Plus, she helped raise me to be a strong woman who understands the importance of investing and building wealth.

Cailin, for always being excited, supportive, and loving. But more so for being an amazing example of what you can achieve when you invest in yourself.

Peach, my husband,* who handles so much of our day-to-day lives when I'm in writing or promotion mode and who provides untold amounts of emotional support.

All my friends, who tolerate (whether in person or via text/FaceTime) the volatile author cycle of excited, hermit-like, stressed out, back to excited, exhausted, terrified, and jumping for joy.

Eric Myers, for always being in my corner and offering sage counsel.

Thank you to my editor, Lauren Appleton, for all the guidance, tweaking, and answering many, many emails.

To Stephanie Bowen for still toasting to next books in the series and

---

*I wrote this book before we actually said "I do," but it was published after our marriage, so it was exciting to be writing "husband" for the first time!

for helping to continue building the strength of the Broke Millennial brand.

Allyssa and Emily, for working tirelessly to help this book make a splash.

A huge thank-you to my interviewees, who made this book possible: Jennifer Barrett, Alex Benke, Douglas Boneparth, Maria Bruno, Dave Fanger, Ashley Fox, Tela Holcomb, Colleen Jaconetti, Sallie Krawcheck, Brandon Krieg, Kelly Lannan, Avi Lele, Dave Nugent, Mabel Nuñez, Jill Schlesinger, Carrie Schwab-Pomerantz, and Julie Virta.

And to the people who helped coordinate those interviews, including Adrianna Abreu, MeeJin Annan-Brady, Stephanie Corns, Katie Davis, Rachael Factor, Allyson Federbush, Meghan Gardler, Lindsay Goldwert, Natalie Rix, Danielle Shechtman, Mike Shamrell, Elyse Steinhaus, Carolyn Wegemann, and Joe Ziemer.

A special shout-out to Tanja Hester, Stefanie O'Connell, Paulette Perhach, Liz Thames, and Kristin Wong for the mastermind (let's be honest, support) groups!

To the personal finance/money nerd community—for all the love and support.

Finally, to the Broke Millennial community and supporters. None of this would be possible without you all.

Notes

INTRODUCTION

1. CPI Inflation Calculator, online tool, Bureau of Labor Statistics, US Department of Labor, https://www.bls.gov/data/inflation_calculator.htm.
2. "CPI: All Urban Consumers," graph, Bureau of Labor Statistics, US Department of Labor, August 28, 2018, https://data.bls.gov/timeseries/CUUR0000S A0L1E?output_view=pct_12mths.
3. "The Rise of the Young Buyer," *The Wall Street Journal*, http://online.wsj.com/ article/SB10001424127887324879504578601711248140752.html

CHAPTER 1

1. Dan Culloton, "A Brief History of Indexing," Morningstar, August 9, 2011, http://news.morningstar.com/articlenet/article.aspx?id=390749.

CHAPTER 2

1. FINRA, "Funds and Fees: Understanding Mutual Fund Fees," FINRA, http:// www.finra.org/investors/funds-and-fees.
2. Dr. Edward Yardeni, Joe Abbott, and Mali Quintana, "Market Briefing: S&P 500 Bull & Bear Markets & Corrections," Yardeni Research Inc., August 24, 2018, https://www.yardeni.com/pub/sp500corrbear.pdf.

CHAPTER 4

1. IRS, "Individual Retirement Arrangements (IRAs)," https://www.irs.gov /retirement-plans/individual-retirement-arrangements-iras.
2. IRS, "Retirement Plans for Self-Employed People," IRS.gov, https://www.irs .gov/retirement-plans/retirement-plans-for-self-employed-people.

3. Board of Governors of the Federal Reserve System, "2017 Federal Reserve Board Report on Economic Well-Being of US Households," press release, May 19, 2017, https://www.federalreserve.gov/newsevents/pressreleases/other/20170519a.htm.
4. Philip L. Cooley, Carl M. Hubbard, and Daniel T. Walz, "Sustainable Withdrawals Rates from Your Retirement Portfolio," at http://afcpe.org/assets/pdf/vol1014.pdf.

CHAPTER 5

1. Real rate from 2015/16 school year.
2. Navient, Loan Repayment Calculator, https://navient.wealthmsi.com/loanrepay.php.
3. Nick Holeman, "Should You Invest, or Pay Off Debt?" Betterment, July 14, 2016, https://www.betterment.com/resources/invest-or-pay-off-debt/.

CHAPTER 6

1. US Securities and Exchange Commission, "Broker-Dealers: Why They Ask for Personal Information," Fast Answers, US SEC, https://www.sec.gov/fast-answers/answersbd-persinfohtm.html.
2. FINRA, "What to Expect When You Open a Brokerage Account," http://www.finra.org/investors/what-expect-when-you-open-brokerage-account.
3. Patricia Oey, "US Fund Fee Study: Average Fund Fees Paid by Investors Continued to Decline in 2016," Morningstar, May 23, 2017, http://corporate1.morningstar.com/researchlibrary/article/810041/us-fund-fee-study--average-fund-fees-paid-by-investors-continued-to-decline-in-2016/.

CHAPTER 7

1. Mark King, "Investments: Orlando Is the Cat's Whiskers of Stock Picking," *The Guardian*, January 13, 2013, https://www.theguardian.com/money/2013/jan/13/investments-stock-picking.

CHAPTER 8

1. Robinhood, "How Robinhood Makes Money," Robinhood.com, December 9, 2014, https://support.robinhood.com/hc/en-us/articles/202853769-How-Robinhood-Makes-Money.

CHAPTER 10

1. United Nations, "Sustainable Development Goals," http://www.undp.org /content/undp/en/home/sustainable-development-goals.html.

CHAPTER 11

1. "Stock Market Crash of October 1929," Social Welfare History Project, VCU Libraries, https://socialwelfare.library.vcu.edu/eras/great-depression /beginning-of-great-depression-stock-market-crash-of-october-1929/.
2. Gary Richardson and Federal Reserve Bank of Richmond, "Banking Panics of 1930–31: November 1930–August 1931," Federal Reserve History, November 22, 2013, https://www.federalreservehistory.org/essays/banking_panics _1930_31.
3. Mark Hulbert, "25 Years to Bounce Back? Try 4 ½," *The New York Times,* April 25, 2009, https://www.nytimes.com/2009/04/26/your-money/stocks-and -bonds/26stra.html.
4. Donald Bernhardt, Marshall Eckblad, and Federal Reserve Bank of Chicago, "Stock Market Crash of 1987," Federal Reserve History, November 22, 2013, https://www.federalreservehistory.org/essays/stock_market_crash_of_1987.
5. NASDAQ Composite Index, graph, "Economic Research," Federal Reserve Bank of St. Louis, https://fred.stlouisfed.org/series/NASDAQCOM/.
6. S&P 500 Composite Index, "Economic Research," Federal Reserve Bank of St. Louis, https://fred.stlouisfed.org/series/SP500.
7. Fred Imbert, "Dow Pops 224 Points, Stocks Notch Record Close on Strong Earnings," January 26, 2018, CNBC, https://www.cnbc.com/2018/01/26/us -stocks-gdp-economy-trump.html.

Index